OSPREY COMBAT AIRCRAFT • 19

SUNDERLAND SQUADRONS
OF WORLD WAR 2

SERIES EDITOR: TONY HOLMES

OSPREY COMBAT AIRCRAFT • 19

SUNDERLAND SQUADRONS
OF WORLD WAR 2

JON LAKE

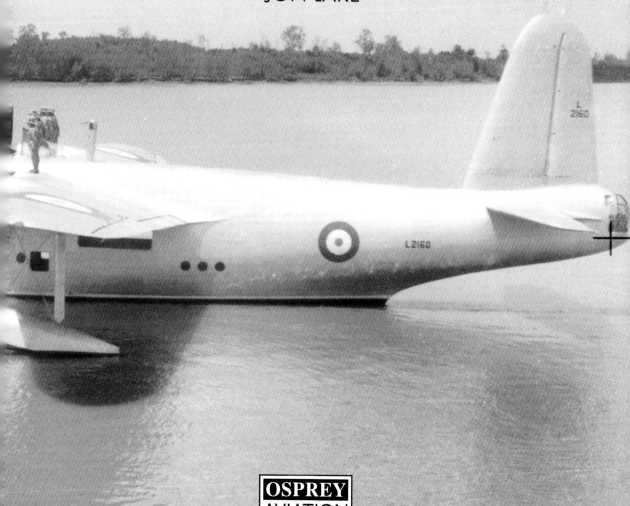

OSPREY
AVIATION

Front cover
This Sunderland Mk III of No 422
'Canadian' Sqn is seen patrolling over
an east-bound convoy out of Halifax,
Novia Scotia, in September 1944.
Formed at the height of the Battle of
the Atlantic in April 1942 at Lough
Erne (later renamed Castle Archdale),
in North Ireland, this unit spent virtu-
ally the entire war patrolling the
Western Approaches from its base
south-west of Omagh. Although this
particular aircraft boasts the later
ASV Mk III radar associated with the
Mk V, it is still powered by a quartet
of venerable Bristol Pegasus engines.
Only when the latter were replaced
by Pratt & Whitney R-1830-9OB Twin
Wasps would the Sunderland's des-
ignation change
(cover artwork by Iain Wyllie)

First published in Great Britain in 2000 by Osprey Publishing,
Elms Court, Chapel Way, Botley, Oxford, OX2 9LP
E-mail: info@ospreypublishing.com

ISBN 1 84176 024 2

Edited by Tony Holmes
Page design by TT Designs, T & B Truscott
Cover Artwork by Iain Wyllie
Aircraft Profiles by Chris Davey
Scale Drawings by Mark Styling
Origination by Grasmere Digital Imaging, Leeds, UK
Printed through Bookbuilders, Hong Kong

00 01 02 03 04   10 9 8 7 6 5 4 3 2 1

EDITOR'S NOTE
To make this best-selling series as authoritative as possible, the editor would be
interested in hearing from any individual who may have relevant photographs,
documentation or first-hand experiences relating to aircrews, and their aircraft,
of the various theatres of war. Any material used will be credited to its original
source. Please write to Tony Holmes at 10 Prospect Road, Sevenoaks, Kent,
TN13 3UA, Great Britain, or by e-mail at: tony.holmes@osprey-jets.freeserve.co.uk

ACKNOWLEDGEMENTS
The Editor wishes to thank Phil Jarrett, Bruce Robertson and Andy Thomas for
providing photographs for use in this volume. Finally, Osprey also acknowledges the
provision of photographs from both the Aerospace Publishing and *Aeroplane*
archives.

CONTENTS

INTRODUCTION

The Sunderland was the longest-serving frontline aircraft of its generation, out-lasting the Spitfire and Mosquito by performing its originally designed role from June 1938 until May 1959. For an aircraft to amass 21 years in frontline service with the RAF was then virtually unheard of, such was the pace of aeronautical change and progress. This is easy to overlook in an era in which the Canberra has already amassed 50 years in service, and the B-52 threatens to go on for perhaps 70 years. Today, 25 years in frontline service is routine, and passes unnoticed, but this is a recent phenomenon, the product of the huge cost of new aircraft and the very slow progress in basic performance. But in the 1940s and 50s a service life of five years was by no means unusual, and during the war, it could be even shorter. So 21 years of frontline RAF service for the Sunderland represented something of a record. The French *Aéronavale* kept the type in service even longer, and in New Zealand the last military Sunderland was only retired in 1965. Finally, a handful of civil Sunderlands kept going into the 1970s. Few aircraft in frontline service at the beginning of the war were still in service even by the end of the conflict, with the Sunderland being arguably the most notable exception.

The Sunderland is widely (and inaccurately) remembered as having provided the mainstay of RAF Coastal Command during World War 2, and as an aircraft of almost legendary prowess in the war against the

Still wearing pre-war colours, with pre-war roundels and even a serial repeated on their rudders, a gaggle of No 210 Sqn Sunderland Is provide an early convoy with close protection. This unit was based at Pembroke Dock, in west Wales, at the time. The aircraft closest to the camera is L2165, which was lost just days after this photograph was taken when it crashed in Milford Haven on 18 September 1939 due to fuel starvation *(via Phil Jarrett)*

The flight deck of an early Sunderland, showing the relative spaciousness and excellent all-round view afforded to the pilots. The lack of flying helmets shows that this is an early, pre-intercom photo (*via Aeroplane*)

No 210 Sqn Sunderland I L2163 shows off the type's forward-hingeing bomb-aimer's window just below the nose turret, as well as a full-height fin-flash and a well-worn coat of camouflage paint. Two crewmen can just be seen in the port upper gun hatch behind the pop-out slipstream deflector. Delivered new to No 210 Sqn in mid-1938, this aircraft survived almost four years of uninterrupted frontline flying, serving with Nos 240, 10 RAAF and 228 Sqns following its spell with the former unit. L2163 sunk at its moorings on 15 January 1942 when a gale battered No 228 Sqn's Stranraer base. It was subsequently salvaged and utilised as an instructional airframe (*Author's collection*)

U-Boat. This campaign is itself remembered as being one of great excitement, frequent acts of insane bravery and fierce action in which the Sunderlands played a pivotal part. A body of mythology has grown up around the Sunderland, over-stating the effectiveness of its defensive armament, over-estimating its ability to land on and take off from open water and over-emphasising its numerical and proportional importance within Coastal Command's order of battle.

In fact the Sunderland was a vitally important Coastal Command asset throughout the war, but it was never as important numerically as the Command's land-based long range patrol aircraft, and was never as efficient a submarine killer as many of its rivals, including the Command's

other principal flying boat, the US Consolidated Catalina. But it was British, and as such attracted greater attention from the Ministry of Information, the RAF's own publicity machine (such as it was), 'Fleet Street' and the specialist magazines, although such attention was always fairly limited, with the publicists and propagandists preferring to concentrate on the more obviously glamorous Fighter Command and the more obviously heroic men of Bomber Command.

Coastal Command fulfilled an equally vital role, but its achievements were seldom very visible, its greatest successes indicated by a convoy coming through without loss, or with minimal losses. Simply preventing the enemy from fulfilling his aims is seldom easy to present in an up-beat way, and is hard to quantify and explain in a way in which the public would understand. Far easier to scroll out lists of how many fighters had been shot down by our own fighters, or to detail the tonnage of bombs dropped on this city or that.

The Sunderland served in a campaign which even many of its participants remember as being filled with hour after hour of mind-crushing tedium and monotony, during which many crews completed tours of operations without ever encountering the enemy. One former Sunderland squadron CO, Wg Cdr L G J Archambault of No 423 Sqn, later commented that, 'I flew like a son-of-a-gun, never saw anything, never shot at anything, nobody shot at me and I never saw a German'. Many Coastal Command crews would have similar recollections. But uneventful did not mean the same as pointless or unproductive, and the fact that Coastal Command went on flying its patrols day in, day out, had a devastating effect on the enemy's ability to wage war.

Morale in the Sunderland units was usually high, despite everything, and the force cultivated its own distinct identity. Sunderland squadrons revelled in their isolation from the RAF's traditional inland aerodromes,

Late-production Sunderland III EJ164 taxies during pre-delivery tests in November 1943. The aircraft's radar antenna fit has not been completed, and squadron markings have yet to be applied. This Mk III would eventually serve with No 308 Flying Boat Training Unit (FTU), followed by No 270 Sqn – the latter unit was then based in British West Africa (now Nigeria). EJ164 was lost whilst still assigned to No 270 Sqn when its crew was forced to ditch in the South Atlantic on 3 October 1944 *(via Phil Jarrett)*

and the unprecedented comfort of the spacious and well-appointed Sunderlands with their galleys and bunks led crews to regard their aircraft as homes-from-home when on detachment – and sometimes even at base! They were an enormous improvement over the cramped, wet, cold and inhospitable biplane boats which had gone before, and their proud crews went to great lengths to emphasise their nautical leanings. Cap badges and uniform buttons were often left deliberately unpolished to encourage the formation of verdigris, and the attire of a typical Sunderland crew often bore more resemblence to that of a fishing boat crew than of an RAF bomber crew. And Sunderland captains only baulked at growing beards due to RAF regulations. Great pride was taken in seamanship, and it was no coincidence that RAF Mount Batten would become the home of the air force's sailing association – founded by Sunderland aircrew.

The Sunderland itself was a far from perfect aircraft, with many weaknesses alongside its undoubted strengths, hugely vulnerable to enemy defensive fire, to fighters and to the might and power of the sea itself. But in gently steering the reader away from the propaganda-fuelled and over-simplistic view of the Sunderland as the 'war-winning', unmatched and unmatchable 'Flying Porcupine', this author would want to stress his admiration for the men who flew the Sunderlands, who carried out a difficult and often unglamorous task with quiet professionalism, undaunted determination and steady courage.

It must be remembered that the aircraft which they flew (and loved) was sometimes their saviour, but was sometimes almost as great a danger to them as it was to the enemy, and this makes their heroism even more remarkable, and the story of the Sunderland even more fascinating. And if the weather, tiredness and mechanical unreliability sometimes presented a greater enemy to the Sunderland aircrew than did the Germans, that does not detract one iota from their achievements.

Usually remembered as a key weapon in the Battle of the Atlantic, the Sunderland also played a vital role in the war in the Far East, where this No 230 Sqn Mk III was photographed taking off in 1944. Serving exclusively with this unit from late 1942 until it was struck off charge in March 1945, EJ143 has the rear fuselage masts associated with the ASV Mk III radar but no mid-upper gun turret. At the time this photograph was taken, No 230 Sqn was based at Koggala, on the south coast of Ceylon (now Sri Lanka), and was operating detachments at Diego Garcia, Addu Atoll, Kelai and Lake Indawgyi *(via Phil Jarrett)*

PRELUDE TO WAR

Between the wars, the RAF relied on a succession of ungainly looking biplane flying boats for maritime patrol duties, though their role tended to be as much about colonial policing, 'showing the flag' and anti-piracy patrols, as it was about Fleet co-operation and anti-submarine warfare. Felixstowe F 5s gave way to Supermarine Southamptons from 1925, Short Rangoons and Blackburn Irises from 1930, Short Singapores and Blackburn Perths from 1934, Supermarine Scapas from 1935, Saro Londons from 1936 and Supermarine Stranraers from 1937, with the smaller Saro Cloud amphibian used as a trainer for flying boat aircrew.

Most of these types were derived from civilian flying boat airliners used by Imperial Airways on the so-called 'Empire Routes', and by the mid-1930s were looking increasingly anachronistic. Just as the old fabric-covered (and sometimes wooden) biplane bombers and fighters gave way to modern all-metal monoplanes during the 1930s, so too it was decided that the biplane flying boats should be replaced by modern monoplane flying boats. Air Ministry Specification R.2/33 called for a four-engined monoplane flying boat to replace the larger of the various biplanes, and resulted in the construction of competing prototypes by Shorts and Saunders Roe. Saro's aircraft suffered an accident, leaving the Short aircraft (a relative but not a derivative of the C-Class 'Empire' Flying Boat airliner) as the de facto winner.

But Short's victory was more than a result of pure serendipity. The company had been late in designing its own flying boats (thanks to the opposition of Horace, the oldest of the three Short brothers), but had gained massive experience building its own floatplanes and Felixstowe-

The first Sunderland prototype (then still known as the S 23) is seen here in its original configuration, with unswept wing and original step. Photographed on the slipway at Short's Rochester plant, K4774 made its maiden flight on 16 October 1937. The aircraft remained with the MAEE until it was finally struck off charge in 1944 (via Phil Jarrett)

The second production Sunderland was L2160, which is seen here showing off the swept wing fitted to production aircraft. This modified configuration was the cause of the Sunderland's distinctive outward-canted engines. The aircraft was photographed during fuel jettison trials conducted by the RAF on 3 June 1938 off the Suffolk coast. L2160 departed for No 230 Sqn, based at Seletar, in Singapore, shortly after this sortie, arriving at its new home on 4 July. This aircraft eventually returned to the UK in late 1941, being issued to No 4 (Coastal) Operational Training Unit (OTU) at Invergordon, in northern Scotland, before year end. It subsequently remained with the training unit as a maintenance airframe long after it was eventually grounded *(via Aeroplane)*

designed flying boats. It had also pioneered all-metal construction with the Silver Streak, which used neither wood nor fabric in its construction, and an experimental metal-hulled Felixstowe F 5. Since World War 1, Short's six Rangoons and 37 Singapores (plus seven civil Calcuttas and three four-engined Kents) had put the company at the forefront of flying boat manufacture. By comparison, rivals Blackburn built four Irises and four Perths, while Supermarine built 66 Southamptons, although the latter were anachronistic with open cockpits, and early aircraft had wooden hulls and straight wings. Supermarine built only 14 of the more modern Scapas for the RAF, and 23 Stranraers.

But quite apart from the number of Short boats built for the RAF and Imperial Airways, the Kent-based company was also at the forefront of advanced flying boat design, demonstrating its prowess with the one-off R.24/31 'Knuckleduster' of 1934 – this all-metal, gull-winged aircraft was powered by two steam-cooled Rolls-Royce Goshawk engines. Finally, the firm also constructed the huge six-engined Sarafand of 1932.

What became the Sunderland owed a great deal to a 1934 Imperial Airways requirement for an improved and enlarged Kent flying boat to serve the newly-announced Empire Air Mail scheme, under which the airline expected to use flying boats on all of its major trunk routes. Despite its later S 25 designation, the design which became the Sunderland was actually started before that of the Imperial Airways S 23, following the issue of Air Ministry Specification R.2/33 on 23 November 1933.

Neither the Air Ministry nor Imperial Airways specified that their new aircraft should be monoplanes, but adoption of the monoplane configuration became inevitable after the 1934 Empire Air Race, in which the Douglas DC-2 performed with great distinction, impressing Oswald Short (the company chairman) and his chief designer Arthur Gouge.

L2160 and three of its sister-Sunderlands within No 230 Sqn were purchased for the RAF by the Federated Malay Sultanates. To denote their 'local' connection, the quartet of flying boats were named by each of the Sultans from the federation, L2160 being christened *Selangor* by His Royal Highness at Port Swettenham in October 1938. This photograph was taken during the ceremony, and although the name on the Sunderland's nose is still covered by the Sultan's personal standard, No 230 Sqn's 'Tiger Beer' badge is just visible below the cockpit *(via Phil Jarrett)*

In 1939, what passed for a detailed caption on the back of this print, taken by a staff photographer from *The Aeroplane*, read simply 'A Coastal Command Sunderland flying-boat on patrol'! The use of large single-letter code letters was discontinued when unit badges were removed after Munich *(via Phil Jarrett)*

Once that decision had been made, Short used the four-engined Scion Senior floatplane to provide the basis of the larger civil S 23 and military S 25, starting out by simply doubling the Scion Senior's dimensions, and adding retractable trailing edge flaps to make up for the rather higher wing loading. The Short design team shaved 18 inches from the 11 ft 6-in beam dictated for the planing bottom by the '3rootW' law, and compensated for the narrowness of the cabin by providing a two-deck layout.

The S 23 and S 25 were developed in parallel, and thus shared many features in common, with similarly advanced construction and low-drag design, while still managing to avoid complex, labour-intensive and expensive double-curvature to an astonishing extent. The design also used joggled joints in the Alclad skin, and counter-sunk flush rivets.

Imperial Airways were impressed enough to order 14 'Empire' Class (or C Class) flying boats off the drawing board, subsequently increasing the £1.75m order to 28, without waiting for the result of prototype trials. The RAF were unable to take such a bold step, and spent longer examining the Short proposal on the drawing board, considering alternative armament schemes, including four gunners' cockpits each with a single 0.303-in Lewis gun, and with provision for a forward-firing 37 mm COW gun in the bows, or two vertical COW guns in the belly. Eventually the RAF settled on power-operated single-gun FN 11 and four-gun FN 13 turrets in the nose and tail, respectively, with provision for single Vickers K-guns firing through cut-outs in the upper sides of the fuselage.

The provision of the power-operated four-gun rear turret altered the centre of gravity considerably, and led to the provision of a swept-back wing (with outward canted engines) on production Sunderlands. The aircraft's offensive armament (consisting of four 500-lb bombs or eight 250-lb bombs) was loaded on carriers suspended from

rollers mounted in box beams which extended out from the centreline of the top-decking and through the inboard sections of the mainplanes. This allowed the bombs to be swung out under the inner wings using a worm and rack mechanism coupled to hand-operated winches.

All of these changes meant that while the first S 23 (G-ADHL *Canopus*, which was not strictly a prototype) made its maiden flight on 3 July 1936, the S 25 prototype (K4774) did not emerge from the No 3 shop at Rochester until 14 October 1937, and did not fly until 16 October. This aircraft, which could be regarded as the Sunderland prototype, initially retained an unswept straight wing, and lacked any of the other changes associated with the changed centre of gravity. These changes included moving the main step further aft (then re-tailoring it to restore hydrodynamic performance). The aircraft was also powered by 950 hp Bristol Pegasus X engines, rather than the planned 1010 hp Pegasus XXIIs.

John Lankester Parker and his co-pilot, Harold Piper, found the aircraft wholly satisfactory, apart from the expected tail heaviness, and after a short series of flights K4774 went back into the workshops to receive the swept back wing and hull modifications. The aircraft re-emerged and flew again on 7 March 1938.

But even while the S 25 prototype began trials, the Air Ministry was eager to 'make up time' and get the Sunderland into service as soon as possible. A first production batch of Sunderland Is (L2158 to L2168) was therefore ordered immediately.

The first production aircraft had the Sunderland's characteristic swept wing and canted outward engines, and the revised step and hull. Compared to the civil C-Class, the Sunderland had a hull with a deeper forefoot, a tapered rear step (fairing to vertical knife edge) and with the flight deck set further aft to leave room for the bow turret, which was itself retractable on the surface to leave a space for a crewman to supervise mooring. Weighing in at 44,600 lb (all up), 85 ft 8 in long and spanning

No 230 Sqn's L2164 *Pehang* is refuelled using cans of Shell Aviation Spirit whilst swinging at its mooring in late 1938. Completing such a task in the sweltering heat of the Far East was hard work, as the fuel had to be man-handled from the canoe onto the flying boat, and then carried from the nose, through the fuselage and up to the wing, where the tanks were filled by hand. Transferred to No 228 Sqn in 1940, L2164 suffered a spectacular demise in Malta's St Paul's Bay on 10 March 1941, when it was set ablaze by strafing Bf 109Es from 7./JG 26 – see chapter four, page 76 *(via Phil Jarrett)*

112 ft 8 in, the Sunderland I was powered by four Bristol Pegasus XXII engines, each rated at 1010 hp, and driving de Havilland-built Hamilton two-pitch three-bladed airscrews. This powerplant allowed a top speed of 210 mph (at 6500 ft), and the aircraft cruised at 178 mph.

Of aluminium-coated, anodised light alloy construction, the Sunderland's hull was built up around a centre keelson with channel-section vertical frames slotted to fit over it and interconnected by longitudinal intercostal 'Z'-section stiffeners. Rivets on the external surfaces were countersunk to reduce drag.

The forward fuselage had double decks, with the wardroom and main entrance door below the flight deck. Forward of this was the mooring compartment (on a raised deck) containing the anchor, its winch, a J-Type dinghy and the mooring ladder. In the front of the compartment was a forward hinging bomb-aimer's window and bomb-sight. Aft of the wardroom was the galley, which contained the drogue stowage compartments as well as the standard culinary equipment – standard only for the Sunderland, that is!

Three Sunderlands cavort for an audience of bowler-hatted VIPs, most of whom appear to be watching with some interest. In the war which would soon follow, Sunderlands usually operated alone (via Aeroplane)

The Clyde Cooker comprised an oven between two primus stoves, with two heating rings, and there was 25 gallons of fresh water literally 'on tap'. A sink was even provided for washing up. At the aft end of the lower deck were the crew quarters, with two bunks and a table in the forward compartment, and two bunks in the rear. The Sunderland had a proper, flushing water closet (with an 11-gallon tank), with a wash-basin and shaving mirror. Behind this was a catwalk to the rear gun turret. Access to the flight deck was via a companionway adjacent to the main entrance door, or a ladder in the galley. A catwalk led from the flight engineer's station aft to the mid-gunners' platforms. On later versions, with a power-operated mid-upper turret, this catwalk was replaced by a companionway.

The flight deck accommodated the pilot and co-pilot side-by-side, each with a massive wheel-type control column, the top of which could hinge down to provide an unobstructed view of the fairly rudimentary instruments (ASI, altimeter, gyro-compass and gyro-horizon, rate of climb indicator and turn and slip indicator, with boost and rpm gauges for the engines). The aircraft was fitted with a Mk IV 3-axes autopilot.

The wings were of all-metal cantilever construction, built around a main spar. This was formed by two pairs of tapering T-shaped extrusions braced vertically and diagonally to form a front and rear truss. The wings each contained three fuel tanks, resting on wooden grids fitted between

N9021 of No 202 Sqn is gently eased down the slipway at its Kalafrana base, on Malta, in May 1939. This aircraft was the first example of the Shorts flying boat delivered to the unit, which was equipped with Saro London IIs at the time. Arriving in April, the Sunderland spent only a few weeks with No 202 Sqn, for the conversion was cancelled the following month and the aircraft was sent to No 228 Sqn instead. N9021 had briefly served with the MAEE prior to its allocation to No 202 Sqn, and it subseqently flew with Nos 204 and 201 Sqns. It was finally written off in a landing accident at Invergordon on 15 December 1940 whilst still a part of No 201 Sqn, the pilot stalling the Sunderland during the final moments of his approach. The aircraft lost one of its floats in the impact, causing it to capsize and sink *(via Andy Thomas)*

the bottom booms and accessed via cut-outs in the top surfaces. One tank was located between the root and the inboard engines, another between the engines and the last outboard of the outer engines. All-metal wing-tip floats were mounted on dual struts below the outer wings, braced by streamlined wires. The wings and flaps were metal-skinned, but the ailerons had fabric covered trailing edges. The tail surfaces were attached to the fuselage by bolts in expanding bushes, and had control surfaces which were primarily fabric-covered.

The first of the production Sunderlands made its maiden flight on 21 April 1938, and was delivered to the Marine Aircraft Experimental Establishment (MAEE) at Felixstowe for exhaustive service trials on 25 April 1938. Here, it joined K4774, which had been sent to the MAEE 17 days earlier, while L2159 arrived at Felixstowe on 9 May. But even before such trials were over, two Sunderlands (L2159 and L2160) were ferried out to No 230 Sqn in Singapore, arriving on 22 June and 4 July, by No 210 Sqn crews, who returned with the first of the unit's discarded Singapores. The rest of the first production batch went to No 210 Sqn at Pembroke Dock as temporary replacements for that unit's Singapores. Three of the aircraft (L2161, L2164 and L2166) were soon diverted to No 230 Sqn, where four of the first five were named after the Federated Malay Sultanates which had paid for them (L2160 *Selangor*, L2161 *Negri-Sembilan*, L2164 *Pehang* and L2166 *Perak*).

No 210 Sqn had received nine aircraft by the end of November 1938, while No 202 Sqn (intended to be the second UK-based Sunderland unit) received two aircraft in April 1939, for crew training. No 230 Sqn

had, meanwhile, been brought up to full strength with the delivery of its eighth aircraft on 16 January 1939. In the event, No 202's conversion to the Sunderland was cancelled, and its aircraft were transferred to No 228 Sqn, which officially began to re-equip in November 1938. It subsequently moved out to Alexandria in June 1939. The final pre-war RAF Sunderland unit to form was No 204 Sqn, which began conversion at Mount Batten in June 1939.

On the outbreak of war, the RAF had 38 Sunderlands on charge, two more having been written off in accidents. L2162 of No 210 Sqn had been lost in a night landing accident on 20 September 1938, while L5801 was lost immediately after taking off from the Johore Straits on 5 June 1939. Four crew had been killed in the latter crash, although the pilot, Flg Off W W Campbell, survived. He would later sink two Italian submarines on consecutive days in June 1940, flying No 230 Sqn's L5804.

More Sunderlands were coming off the assembly line, but the next batch were ear-marked for the Royal Australian Air Force (RAAF). No 10 (General Reconnaissance) Sqn was officially formed at Point Cook, Victoria, on 1 July 1939 with the intention that it would become a home-based maritime unit to be based at Rathmines, in New South Wales. Seven pilots (and a small party of other air- and groundcrew) were sent to the UK to convert to the aircraft, gain experience, and then receive and prepare the newly ordered aircraft for ferrying back to Australia in October 1939.

The pilots converted to the Sunderland at Calshot, then joined the other personnel at Pembroke Dock, where they were attached to the RAF's No 210 Sqn. The first aircraft were collected from Shorts in September 1939, but four RAAF pilots were loaned to RAF units for operational duties, and the decision was then taken that the Australian Sunderland squadron would remain in Britain to participate in operations, and the rest of the unit was transferred out from Australia.

This was fortuitous, since No 10 Sqn (RAAF) was destined to become one of the most distinguished and successful of all the wartime Sunderland units. And war was about to break out.

L5802 of Mount Batten-based No 204 Sqn is seen 'on the step' during its take off run in Plymouth Sound. The aircraft has two-letter identification codes and toned-down fuselage roundels – the central white 'ring' has been overpainted in blue. With the rest of the airframe finished in silver dope, there seems to have been little point in such toning-down of the national marking. Prior to serving with No 204 Sqn, this aircraft had spent time with No 210 Sqn, and it would go on to fly with Nos 201, 95 and 461 (RAAF) Sqns, and No 4 OTU. L5802 was finally written off in a night landing at Alness, near Invergordon, on 16 January 1943 whilst still attached to the training unit (via Phil Jarrett)

SUNDERLAND GOES TO WAR

On the outbreak of war Coastal Command had Nos 210 and 204 Sqns (at Pembroke Dock and Mount Batten) on its books, with No 230 Sqn in the Far East and No 228 in Egypt. Something of a bonus was the continued presence of No 10 Sqn (RAAF), which had been intended to transfer back to Australia in October, and which was ordered to stay in Britain and participate in operations from its adopted base at Pembroke Dock. It thus became the first Dominion squadron to operate in Europe during World War 2, and would be the only Commonwealth unit to fly continuously on operations from 1940 to 1945.

No 10 Sqn flew its first operational flight (ferrying a spare engine out to Bizerta for No 228 Sqn) on 10 October 1939, although it was initially a lodger unit, and was not officially declared operational. The unit was formally incorporated into Coastal Command's No 15 Group on 3 January 1940, and flew its first official war sortie on 6 February 1940, although many of the unit's pilots had already been flying operationally on loan to Nos 210 and 228 Sqns. One such individual was Flt Lt Charles W Pearce, who captained this, the first sortie of World War 2 manned by an all-Australian crew – the aircraft involved was P9605/K. Promoted to squadron leader by the summer, Pearce was later awarded the RAAF's first DFC since the inception of the service in 1921. The *London Gazette* ran the following announcement to mark the award in its 30 July 1940 edition;

'This officer has consistently displayed gallantry and devotion to duty whilst engaged on convoy and anti-submarine patrols. In June 1940, Sqn Ldr Pearce attacked an enemy submarine off the coast of Portugal, one bomb being observed to burst near the bow. This officer has displayed courage and resource in anti-submarine work and, by his personal energy and skill, has formed the squadron into a highly efficient operational unit.'

While the Australians were relatively slow to start flying war sorties, other units were sent into the breach straight away. No 210 Sqn claimed the honour of making the first Sunderland sortie of the war, as Flt Lt Allan Ainslie was already airborne (having taken off from Pembroke Dock at

This photograph seems to offer conclusive proof that at least one Sunderland I was painted with black undersides. N9028 flew exclusively with No 204 Sqn, which used the codes 'RF' and then 'KG'. This aircraft was downed by Bf 110s near Trondheim on 21 July 1940 *(via Aeroplane)*

0500) in L2165/B when Prime Minister Neville Chamberlain made his famous announcement to the nation at 1100 on the morning of 3 September 1939. The sortie was destined to be typical of most of the Sunderland missions which followed – cold and entirely uneventful. Ainslie, who was awarded a DFC in February 1940, was lost in action in June. On 4 September 1939 No 210's Flt Lt Harrison had a more eventful patrol, coming under fire from friendly AA guns. Fortunately, his aircraft, L5799/D, escaped unscathed.

The Sunderlands commenced convoy patrols within days of war being declared, for the merchant navy had immediately responded to the potential U-Boat threat by moving *en masse* in an effort to gain better protection from the enemy. These convoys initially sailed along the east coast and then, from 7 September, across the Atlantic itself. Sunderlands (which would be Coastal Command's longest ranging aircraft until the introduction of Liberators and Catalinas in early 1941) remained with the convoys until they were about 100 miles west of the Scillies. Some units even briefly sent detachments to Brest and Falmouth to try and stretch the cover further into the Atlantic, but this was not enough, for 39 of the 58 U-Boats then in service had slipped undetected into the Atlantic during August 1939.

No 210 Sqn claimed the first attack on an enemy submarine on 8 September when Flt Lt Hyde's crew sighted and attacked two submarine periscopes south west of the Lizard. None of the eight bombs dropped had any obvious effect, however.

The next wartime incident in which the Sunderland was involved was the rescue of the crew of the tramp-steamer *Kensington Court*, which had been shelled by a surfaced U-Boat about 70 miles from the Scillies. It marked the first major operation for No 228 Sqn, which had been ordered back from Alexandria on 8 September 1939. The unit flew home

Photographs of new Sunderlands being launched are regrettably uncommon, not least because production during the early years failed to keep pace with the need for aircraft – and even with the rate of losses *(via Phil Jarrett)*

to Pembroke Dock, but had lost one aircraft within 48 hours of returning to Wales when, on 10 September, a Sunderland damaged its wing floats while landing downwind at nearby Angle Bay. The flying boat was quickly placed under tow, but subsequently turned turtle and sank before it could reach the safety of Pembroke Dock.

Even with four Sunderland units now patrolling home waters (Nos 204, 201, 228 and 10 RAAF Sqns), the number of aircraft physically available was very small – perhaps two-dozen serviceable aeroplanes at any one time. These were split between Mount Batten and Pembroke Dock, the Sunderlands flying convoy escort patrols and ASW sweeps over the North-West and South-West Approaches as part of No 15 Group.

Returning to the *Kensington Court* incident, on 18 September two No 228 Sqn aircraft had picked up the ship's SOS, and the first Sunderland to arrive on the scene was the flying boat captained by Flt Lt Thurstan Smith. He landed close to the ship's liferaft (to which 34 survivors were clinging) and picked up 21 of them, ferrying men from the raft to the aircraft four or five at a time in the Sunderland's two dinghies – he was fearful that the raft itself might puncture the aircraft's hull if he got too close to it. A second Sunderland, flown by Flt Lt John Barratt, then flew an ASW sweep before landing to pick up the remaining survivors.

For a flying boat like the Sunderland to land on the open sea like this may seem to the layman to be nothing extraordinary, but this is far from the truth. The Sunderland's hull was a mere one-sixteenth of an inch thickness of duralumin and was never intended to withstand the pounding of ocean waves and swells. And although many Sunderland Captains would land on the water to rescue downed aircrew and survivors (No 10 Sqn RAAF alone logging 117 such rescues), it was always an extremely risky practise, requiring an extraordinary degree of bravery.

Many such landings went wrong, with the CO of No 461 Sqn providing a typical example on 11 August 1942. His aircraft was badly damaged on attempting to land, being thrown back into the air only to slump down onto the sea. All of the crew got out, but all but one were then drowned. However, the Wellington crew they had gone to the aid of, and the sole survivor from the Sunderland, were subsequently rescued.

On 9 July 1941, Flt Lt Gil Thurstun and his crew were rather luckier, merely losing their starboard underwing float and port outer engine and nacelle, which were ripped off by the impact with the sea. With crew-members on the starboard wingtip to prevent the aircraft from rolling over, Thurstun picked up the Hudson crew he'd landed to help, and they were given

Sunderlands may have failed to make a major dent in U-Boat numbers, but the presence of the big flying boats over the convoys did dramatically reduce the losses of Allied shipping *(via Phil Jarrett)*

hot bacon and eggs from the galley. Thurstun then began to water-taxi towards the Scillies (a 45 hour journey at 3 knots!), but was picked up by British destroyers, which took him and his crew aboard and then sank the Sunderland with their guns. Both of the captains involved in the *Kensington Court*'s rescue were subsequently awarded DFCs, attending an investiture at Buckingham Palace on 2 November 1940. But these awards were a morale-boosting exercise which covered a painful truth – the U-Boats had sent 41 ships (totalling 153,800 tons) to the bottom in the first month of the war.

And on the very day that Thurstan Smith and John Barratt donned their best blues for their day at the Palace, there was a demonstration that the war against Germany's surface raiders was no more effective when the *Deutschland* evaded No 228 Sqn's Sunderlands, and slipped back into the Baltic after a successful foray. And even after the positions of *Scharnhorst* and *Gneisenau* were reported by one of their victims, they too managed to slip home without being detected by searching No 228 Sqn Sunderlands.

For many months, flying boat attacks on U-Boats were inconclusive, not least because the bombs carried were not really suited to anti-submarine use, and since no existing depth charge could be carried by the Sunderland. This was conclusively demonstrated on 3 December 1939 when the submarine HMS *Snapper* was enthusiastically attacked by an RAF aircraft, which scored a direct hit on the conning tower with a standard 100-lb AS bomb. This shattered four electric light bulbs in the submarine's control room, but caused no further damage, except to some crockery.

The 250-lb AS bomb was better, but still needed to score a direct hit, or to explode within six feet of the pressure hull to stand any real chance of causing significant damage. This was demonstrated during other accidental 'Blue on Blue' engagements in the first days of the war. There was no reason to suppose that the same bombs would be any more effective against a U-Boat, and the chance of accurate delivery was made unlikely by the lack of distributors for accurate spacing of sticks of bombs, or effective low-level bombsights.

But there weren't many attacks recorded by the Sunderlands in any case, for they were already seriously over-stretched, tasked with reconnaissance sorties aimed at detecting enemy surface raiders, convoy escort

Australian-manned No 10 Sqn RAAF was one of the first units to use the Sunderland in combat, rapidly gaining a formidable reputation for operational efficiency and great fighting spirit. The disc below the windscreen is a gas detection patch *(via Phil Jarrett)*

and ASW co-operation. Several other Coastal Command units were still equipped with even less effective biplane flying boats, including Saro Londons and Supermarine Stranraers.

At the same time the U-Boat menace was fortunately somewhat over-stated, with only 27 vessels actually fit for operations on the day that war broke out. But the rather limited size of the fleet was not immediately obvious, with Fritz Lemp's U-30 sinking the liner *Athenia* on the first day of the war, U-39 attacking the *Ark Royal* on 14 September and U-29 sinking HMS *Courageous* three days later. It began to look as though the U-Boats were having it all their own way.

Finally, however, on 30 January 1940, ML882/Y of No 228 Sqn (captained by Flt Lt E J Brooks) attacked and damaged the Type VIIB U-Boat U-55, which had already been damaged by Royal Navy ships, and which was then scuttled by its captain. The U-Boat sank, and the kill was shared between No 228 Sqn and the naval ships involved. This was the first sinking of a U-Boat even partly credited to a Sunderland, and it came after 57 sightings and a number of unsuccessful attacks.

At the end of March, two of the Sunderland units were re-located, with No 10 Sqn RAAF moving from Pembroke Dock to Mount Batten, and with No 204 Sqn vacating the Plymouth base for Sullom Voe, in the Shetlands, where it came under No 18 Group control. Here it began covering the gap between Norway and Iceland through which the U-Boats slipped en-route to their patrol areas in the Atlantic. Accommodation at Sullom Voe was primitive (mainly in Nissen Huts), with the No 100 Wing HQ aboard the depot ship *Manela* moored just offshore.

In April, No 201 Sqn at Sullom Voe began trading its obsolete Londons for Sunderlands, later moving to Invergordon at the end of September, with eight aircraft on strength.

April and May 1940 saw the British occupation of the Danish Faroe Isles and the invasion of neutral Iceland, denying Germany two potentially useful U-Boat bases, and providing Coastal Command and the RN with useful bases from which to prosecute their anti-submarine campaign following the denial of similar facilities in neutral Eire.

On the debit side, Hitler invaded Norway to secure iron ore supplies to the Ruhr, the invasion force being sighted first (on 8 April) by a No 204 Sqn Sunderland (N9047). Aircraft from the other UK-based Sunderland units had been detached to Sullom Voe for several weeks previously, and had also flown patrols off the Norwegian coast. On the same day that approaching German force was located, No 204 Sqn lost L5799/D (captained by Flt Lt R P A Harrison) in an encounter with a He 111H from 1(F)./122. Two days later No 210 Sqn's L2167 (flown by Flt Lt P W H Kite) was shot down by a Bf 110C from 1./ZG 76. Only one crewman survived these two incidents.

Throughout the Norwegian campaign, Sunderlands saw frequent use as transport aircraft, shuttling in vital supplies and senior personnel, and evacuating the wounded. Often, this meant flying into Fjords during enemy air attacks – an occupation that became almost a habit for Flt Lt Robert Craven of No 228 Sqn, and his aircraft, N9025.

After an uneventful flight to Namsos (where Flt Lt Skey had come under attack on 15 April while landing Gen de Wiart and his staff) on 25 April, Craven flew RAF personnel to Aandalsnes two days later.

21

He landed his aircraft in Molde Fjord, and his passengers transferred to HMS *Witherington*. Craven, who had landed during a bombing raid by 12 Ju 88s, went ashore with his passengers in search of orders, leaving his co-pilot, (Plt Off L L Jones) to taxy the aircraft around in an effort to avoid the bombs! When his engines began to overheat, Jones took off, only to be attacked by a Bf 110, which his gunners promptly shot down. Once the Luftwaffe had vacated the area, the co-pilot landed and picked up Craven, before flying on to Aandalsnes, where the flying boat was forced to drift overnight due to there being no anchorage or mooring available.

The Norwegian campaign also witnessed the incident on which the Sunderland's supposed reputation as 'die fliegende Stachelschwein' ('the flying porcupine') was based. The slow, lumbering Sunderland was a large and easy target for enemy aircraft, and although 23 are known to have been shot down by enemy aircraft (plus the majority of the 23 recorded simply as 'failing to return' or 'missing in action'), there were a few occasions when the Sunderland turned the tables on its attackers.

On 3 April 1940, Flt Lt Frank Phillips of No 204 Sqn, flying N9046, did just that. The aircraft, on routine convoy escort, was first attacked by two Ju 88s which were driven off, and then the Sunderland repelled four more as they tried to dive-bomb the convoy. The flying boat was then attacked by a gaggle of six more Ju 88s, which engaged the Sunderland from astern as Phillips manoeuvred at low level. One was shot down by Cpl Bill Lillie in the rear turret, who also put the port engine of the second attacker out of action, forcing the Junkers pilot break off his attack and turn for home, escorted by the four survivors. But even these half-hearted attacks holed every one of the Sunderland's tanks, destroyed its trimming gear and one bomb rack, and injured some of the crew, although it did limp back to Invergordon, winning a DFC for Phillips and a DFM for Lillie.

On 13 July 1940 No 10 Sqn RAAF's Flt Lt 'Hoot' Gibson (flying N9050/D) was attacked by a Bf 110 which his gunners drove off, trailing smoke, after it had holed the Sunderland's tanks. Two days later the same unit's Flt Lt Hugh Birch encountered five He 111s attacking the SS *City of Limerick* south of Bishop's Rock off the Scilly Isles. Birch engaged the

This shot of a No 210 Sqn Sunderland I at its moorings at Oban in May 1940 shows to advantage the conditions under which the groundcrew worked. This aircraft has servicing platforms slung from the wing leading edge, which were standard. If a mechanic dropped his spanner it was generally lost for good, and he would be charged for a replacement! *(via Andy Thomas)*

A weather-beaten L2163 is seen on a convoy patrol from Oban in early 1941. It wears the 'DA' codes of No 210 Sqn *(via Bruce Robertson)*

enemy aircraft, setting one alight and driving off the others. Finally, more than a year later on 14 August 1941, Flt Lt Vic Hodgkinson again of No 10 Sqn RAAF drove off an Fw 200 which left the fight trailing dense smoke and shedding large chunks of debris – an almost certain kill for the lumbering Sunderland.

But the survival of these flying boats, and their success against enemy aircraft, was lucky rather than inevitable, since the Sunderland's armament was pitifully inadequate. Indeed, on other occasions, German aircraft armed with 20 mm cannon simply sat back outside machine gun range and pumped shells into the Sunderlands. Fortunately, the latter was extremely rugged, and could soak up a great deal of punishment – aircraft limped home riddled with bullet and shell holes on numerous occasions.

The Sunderland also enjoyed some unusual design features which enhanced survivability. One of these was the ability for a fitter or flight engineer to crawl out to the engines inside the wing. On at least two occasions this allowed crews to plug and keep topping up damaged oil tanks that meant that engines kept running. The first time this was practised, on 30 June 1941, LAC Milton Griffin of No 10 Sqn RAAF won himself a DFM for his careful husbanding of the port outer engine. A similar incident occurred several months later.

The fall of France in June led to the Germans gaining useful U-Boat bases on the French Atlantic coast from which submarines could reach their patrol areas without having to negotiate the Channel or the North Sea – their most vulnerable areas. This was the beginning of what the U-Boat arm would call *die gluckliche zeit* (the happy time).

The Sunderland force remained small, with slow production just about keeping pace with attrition. But when the U-26 (a rare Type IA) was attacked by Flt Lt Gibson's P9603/H of No 10 Sqn RAAF on 1 July 1940, the Command had only 34 Sunderlands available. The U-Boat (recently depth-charged by HMS *Gladiolus*) was caught on the surface and scuttled by its captain after the Sunderland dropped four 250-lb AS bombs. The kill was shared between the Australins and the RN destroyer.

And these 34 Sunderlands were deployed quite widely, with No 10 Sqn RAAF and No 210 Sqn maintaining detahments at Oban in the same way that units had previously operated from Sullom Voe. Only 20 Sunderlands were delivered to the RAF during 1940, which was a quantity quite insufficient to replace attrition – nine aircraft had been written off during December alone. The UK-based Sunderland force was further depleted when No 228 Sqn returned to the Mediterranean in June 1940, and there were barely enough aircraft to maintain existing units at full strength.

August saw the deployment of ASV Mk I radar on frontline Sunderlands for the first time, initially with No 10 Sqn RAAF. The early radar was unreliable, and offered poor differentiation between different types of target. Along the Spanish and Portuguese coasts, more than one Spanish fishing boat found itself under attack by Sunderlands, whose radar hadn't warned their crews what they were attacking. At least one was bombed, though fortunately with a lack of accuracy. The Australian unit also operated a test aircraft (N9050/D) for the new MDS (Magnetic Detection of Submarines) equipment. This was subsequently abandoned, despite encouraging results from the tests, although it would later form the basis of the MAD (Magnetic Anomaly Detection) system introduced by the Americans later in the war.

But even more significant than radar or MDS were improved weapons. By August 1940, Coastal Command had a stock of about 700 new anti-submarine weapons – standard Mk VII 450-lb Royal Navy depth charges, modified with a rounded aerodynamic nose fairing and tail fins. The Sunderland could carry four of these, which were regarded as being useful and potent ASW weapons. These were later augmented by similarly modified Mk VIII 250-lb depth charges, eight of which could be carried on the racks, with two more carried as 'reloads'.

The first use of these airborne depth charges came on 16 August 1940, when U-51 (a Type VIIB) was attacked by P9624/H of No 210 Sqn, captained by Flt Lt E R Baker. The U-Boat was damaged, but limped home.

The sight of a Sunderland became a real confidence and morale booster for the merchant seamen who crewed the convoys across the Atlantic, since losses were rare while the big flying boats were in the area. This shot was yet another taken by a staff photographer from *The Aeroplane*, who was flying in a second No 210 Sqn Sunderland. The aircraft were protecting a Mediterranean-bound troop convoy *(via Aeroplane)*

'RB' codes identify this low-flying Sunderland as belonging to No 10 Sqn RAAF. Many crews completed their tours of operations without ever seeing an Axis aircraft or submarine, and the biggest enemies were the hours of boredom and the often treacherous weather *(via Aeroplane)*

The next day, Hitler declared a 'total blockade' of the British Isles, announcing that even neutral ships would be attacked on sight. The Luftwaffe's Fw 200 Kondors also began operations, attacking single ships and stragglers, and providing long-range reconnaissance for the U-Boat arm. Shipping losses rose to alarming levels during the autumn and winter – levels which could not be replaced by the ship-builders, and which threatened to cut imports.

The same Flt Lt Baker of No 210 Sqn (again flying P9624/H) was credited with the first unassisted sinking of an enemy submarine by a Sunderland on 6 January 1941 when the Italian boat *Marcello* was claimed sunk 150 miles west of Cape Wrath. In fact the vessel escaped, and was actually lost on 22 February. The first U-Boat (U-31) claimed by an RAF aircraft had been destroyed by a Bomber Command Blenheim (flown by Sqn Ldr Miles Delap of No 82 Sqn) on 11 March 1940.

Baker's success marked something of a 'final fling' for No 210 Sqn's Sunderlands, since the unit converted to the Catalina in April 1941. This conversion was prompted by the continuing shortage of Sunderlands (only 32 were built during the course of that year). With the move of No 204 Sqn from Sullom Voe to Reykjavik in April 1941 (and then to West Africa in July 1941), only two Sunderland units remained in the UK – No 10 Sqn RAAF at Mount Batten and No 201 Sqn at Invergordon. Both units moved base soon afterwards, No 10 to Pembroke Dock in May and No 201 to Lough Erne in Northern Ireland in September. These re-locations marked a shift in emphasis from the North-West and South-West approaches to concentrate on convoy escort deep into the Atlantic itself.

The spring and early summer of 1941 saw a succession of events which marked a turn in the tide of the Battle of the Atlantic, although this was not immediately apparent at the time. Although the tonnage of shipping lost to the U-Boats actually rose (to 294,000, or 43 ships) during the month of April, the U-Boat arm itself lost five submarines, and escort ships refuelled in Iceland were now extending their convoy cover out to 35° West – well over halfway across the ocean.

On 15 April operational control of the Command passed to the Admiralty, enabling much better co-operation with surface forces, and with control being exercised through four Combined Area HQs, the Ops Room at Northwood and the Admiralty submarine tracking room in Whitehall. At the end of 1940, the First Lord of the Admiralty had

requested a massive increase in the strength of shore-based naval co-operation aircraft, suggesting that a minimum of 826 such aircraft were required – an increase of 300 aircraft.

Coastal Command's re-equipment also gathered pace, with aged Stranraers giving way to the first Catalinas in March 1941, and with the last London biplanes (at Gibraltar) replaced by June. Hudsons and Wellingtons began to arrive at the frontline, and more Liberators were earmarked for the Command. The Norwegians (later to become masters of the Sunderland) joined the fight too, with No 330 Sqn initially flying their Northrop N3P-B floatplanes from Iceland, while No 204 Sqn had moved to moorings at Reykjavik in early 1941. But even with these improvements and changes, the aircraft of Coastal Command appeared to have made little contribution to the defeat of the U-Boats. Everyone accepted that the presence of escort aircraft was saving lives, and that patrols were making life more difficult for the U-Boat crews, but U-Boats were not actually being sunk.

This would soon change, however, with the Mk VIII depth charge becoming available in large numbers, and with a switch in tactics away from the valuable deterrent convoy escort missions to real ASW patrols.

German U-Boats en route to their Atlantic patrol areas passed through predictable narrow choke-points, during which they were at their most vulnerable, running at eight knots when submerged (or more usually two knots if battery life were to be conserved) and needing to surface several times every day to re-charge those batteries, and to ventilate the submarine's interior. There were not sufficient aircraft to entirely close the gaps, and at night, or in poor visibility, even a surfaced submarine was hard to detect. Despite these factors, U-Boat sightings (and kills) would soon begin to rise.

The Sunderlands, however, remained largely committed to the convoy escort role, while the Catalinas and later the VLR Liberators prowled the oceans looking for U-Boats, with shorter-range types mounting barrier patrols. Since the outbreak of war, the figures had been somewhat depressing for Coastal Command, with 233 sightings resulting in 164

Sunderland camouflage schemes varied enormously during the early years of the war, as shown by this No 10 Sqn RAAF aircraft, which should be compared with the photos of No 210 Sqn's aircraft featured earlier in this chapter. Rochester-built Mk II W3984 served exclusively with the Australian unit from August 1941 through to December 1943, and was finally struck off charge in July 1944 (via Bruce Robertson)

attacks and only one kill (later disallowed), and two kills shared with Royal Navy surface vessels.

Again, evidence of the up-turn was not obvious, as increased numbers of enemy submarines (including the new ocean-going Type IXs) began to set out on patrol. Allied shipping losses actually rose (to 325,500 tons, or 58 ships) in May, although half of these were sunk by a small group of U-Boats operating in West African waters before No 95 Sqn's three Sunderlands could be reinforced. On 24 May another Sunderland (this time one belonging to No 201 Sqn, captained by Flt Lt Vaughan) witnessed what many regarded as the nadir of the RN's fortunes – the action between British and German capital ships in which HMS *Hood* was blown to pieces by the battleships *Bismarck* and *Prinz Eugen.*

From May 1941, a new Sunderland sub-variant began to arrive in the frontline – the Mk II, powered by two-speed supercharged Pegasus XVIII engines. The new version (Dumbarton-built Sunderland I T9083 was used by Short as a prototype for the improved variant) also added a single Botha-type FN 7 mid-upper turret in place of the usual two open gun hatches. An FN 4a tail turret, with 1000 rpg, also replaced the original FN 13 turret, which had half the ammunition capacity.

More significantly, many of the Mk IIs also introduced ASV Mk II search radar, with Yagi homing aerials under the outer wings, 16 transmitter loops on the sides of the rear fuselage and four characteristic dipole masts above the fuselage. This gave the Sunderland crew a better chance of spotting a submarine conning tower, or even a periscope, although the radar was primitive and performance was poor, except in perfect conditions. But the radar was a useful navaid, especially when returning from a long patrol at night, for it gave a useful picture of the coastline and an accurate indication of the distance from land. This was a real boon, since Sunderland crews still navigated by Dead Reckoning, with the use of sea markers or flame floats to establish drift.

Sunderland Mk I T9072 of No.204 Sqn is seen on its Dunlop beaching trolley at Reykjavik in 1941. The use of bases in Iceland allowed Coastal Command to range much further out over the Atlantic, and helped plugged the gap through which U-Boats could reach their patrol areas. This aircraft later served with No 10 Sqn RAAF, and was written off whilst still assigned to the Australian unit when it crashed into the sea off Holyhead, on the Isle of Anglesey, on 5 December 1941 *(via Bruce Robertson)*

The introduction of radar gave the Sunderland a new tool for finding submarines, although the early ASV equipment was both primitive and of limited performance. Here, a No 204 Sqn Sunderland I is seen festooned with antennas at its Sullom Voe base in late 1941 *(via Andy Thomas)*

The use of a base at Lough Erne in Northern Ireland (together with a corridor through neutral Eire airspace) allowed Coastal Command easier access to the Atlantic. The base, later re-named Castle Archdale, would play a major part in the battle. This No 201 Sqn Sunderland II was photographed at the Northern Ireland base in late 1941 *(via Andy Thomas)*

A total of 75 Sunderland Is were built at Rochester (and 15 more by Blackburn at Dumbarton) before production switched to the new Mk II. Rochester then built 23 Mk IIs (W3976 to W3998), Blackburn five (W6000 to W6004) and Short Brothers and Harland 15 (W6050 to W6064) in Belfast. Although only 43 Mk IIs were constructed, these were eventually spread between Nos 95, 119, 201, 204, 228, 240, 246, 423 and 461 Sqns, and No 10 Sqn RAAF. Fortunately, from an equipment/powerplant standpoint, the Mk II was entirely compatible with the Mk III which followed, if not with the earlier Mk I.

Coastal Command's steadily improving efficiency and capabilities were achieved under the stewardship of AOC-in-C Air Chief Marshal 'Ginger' Bowhill, who was replaced by Sir Philip Joubert on 14 June 1941. Joubert (who had previously led the Command in 1936-37) was soon having to fight his corner as rivalries broke out between his Command and Sir Richard Peirse's Bomber Command, with disagreements over the responsibility for operations in the Channel area.

Joubert was a technocrat, with an unusual grasp of radio and radar for so senior an officer. After a false start during which Joubert favoured the powerful, but fixed, Helmore light over the more flexible Leigh light, the air chief marshal ordered most of the equipment which would eventually win the anti-submarine war, including the aforementioned Leigh light and the Centimetric ASV radar. He even oversaw the camouflage experiments which would see all Coastal Command patrol aircraft being camouflaged like Herring Gulls, with a white belly and grey topsides.

June saw the loss of 61 ships (totalling 310,000 tons) but the totals plummeted in July, dropping to 22 ships and 94,200 tons, and in August Coastal Command managed to sink one U-Boat and capture another, for the loss of 23 ships (80,300 tons). July also saw the USA taking over responsibility for the defence of Iceland, while its ships and aircraft began actively searching for the U-Boats, reporting them in plain language to aid the efforts of both the RN and RAF.

Major convoy battles in September brought the U-Boats more success, with the allies losing 53 ships (202,800 tons), although only three were sunk within 350 miles of a Coastal Command aerodrome! But these losses were partly compensated for by the amendment of the US neutrality act to allow US ships to carry war material to Britain, and by the US Navy's introduction of escorts to two-thirds of the way across the Atlantic. The USA also announced that henceforth it would

attack Axis raiders and submarines, and not just note their position, and all while remaining officially neutral.

Convoys from Britain to Russia began with PQ-1 on 21 August, and these initially suffered no interference. Although U-Boat kills were still a great rarity, the aircraft of Coastal Command did make their presence felt, forcing the submarines to transit as quickly and quietly as possible to their much-restricted operational area in the mid-Atlantic, where they received less help and targeting information from the Fw 200 Kondors. These 40 or so submarines hunting in this area also scored fewer victories of their own than had the nine U-Boats operational in the Atlantic one year before. But preventing losses, and ensuring that more of the convoys got through was not enough to stop criticism of Coastal Command, and Joubert had to fight hard to prevent the transfer of his Whitleys and Wellingtons back to Bomber Command, where they would have been squandered in pointless and largely unproductive night bombing attacks.

The RAF's Sunderlands were heavily committed to the Atlantic battle, with the Australian No 10 Sqn operating from Pembroke Dock in West Wales and No 201 Sqn flying from moorings in Lough Erne, in Northern Ireland. Aircraft operating from Lough Erne (later re-named Castle Archdale, which was the name it had used before February 1941) actually reached the Atlantic via a narrow corridor through neutral Eire's airspace, first used in February 1941.

Both units were occasionally used for other duties, most notably for re-supply missions to Malta and Alexandria, although these diminished as aircraft availability declined. By July, No 10 Sqn RAAF was down to six Sunderlands (plus a single loaned Catalina), while No 201 rarely managed to get more than three aircraft 'on the line' on any one day.

The situation improved slightly in October 1941, with the return of No 228 Sqn from the Mediterranean to Stranraer (and then, from March 1942, Oban). But even with a third UK-based unit, the number of Sunderlands available for operations was less than 24.

Behind the scenes, Short were preparing for a major increase in Sunderland production rates, and would deliver 114 aircraft in 1942. This was still a modest total, and reflected the Air Ministry's timidity in ordering the big flying boat in small batches, and Shorts' pre-occupation with the Stirling heavy bomber for Bomber Command. However, these new aircraft would at least be the first examples of a new and improved Sunderland variant, the Mk III.

The Sunderland Mk III was basically a Mk II with a new faired main step, which decreased drag by about ten per cent without inflicting any loss in hydrodynamic performance. The new faired hull was trialled on the first prototype, K4774, and on the Scion Senior, as well as on T9042, which served as the Mk III prototype – the latter aircraft completed its first flight in its new guise on 28 June 1941. Mk III production began at W3999, which made its maiden flight on 15 December 1941.

In the meantime, November had seen shipping losses drop again to only 62,200 tons (13 ships), although this was partly due to the diversion of 29 U-Boats to the Mediterranean, five of which were sunk en route and five more badly damaged. Operations in the Mediterranean proved extremely successful, with a relay of escort aircraft forcing the waiting U-Boats to stay submerged for so long that they lost contact with their

Radar-equipped Sunderland II W3977 of No 201 Sqn was photographed on patrol from Lough Erne in late 1941. This aircraft is not fitted with the mid-upper gun turret which often distinguished the variant. W3977 was lost on 5 April 1942 when it crashed into the sea near Rathlin Island, off the north Northern Ireland coast *(via Andy Thomas)*

intended targets on at least one occasion. Losses of U-Boats to RAF aircraft also began to rise, although the Sunderland's 'Duck' (in terms of an unassisted, confirmed U-Boat kill) remained unbroken.

No 10 Sqn RAAF's Flt Lt Vic Hodgkinson (whose crew had almost certainly downed an Fw 200 in August) had more luck with a surface ship on 23 December. He attacked an enemy tanker (a mother-ship for U-Boats) in the Bay of Biscay, and despite heavy and accurate flak, left the ship belching smoke and trailing a 600-ft wide oil slick. Hodgkinson then flew his heavily damaged Sunderland home, beaching it at Mount Batten. This was Hodgkinson's 173rd and last trip with the unit, the veteran skipper returning to Australia to fly Catalinas with No 20 Sqn.

The Japanese entered the war in December 1941, and the U-Boat arm took advantage of US unpreparedness by concentrating much of their attention on American coastal waters. They enjoyed a bloody run of successes, accounting for 230,000 tons (40 ships) in just three weeks. Things could have been much worse had Hitler not insisted on maintaining 24 U-Boats off Norway, fearing an allied invasion attempt. The campaign extended into the Caribbean in February, the first 'Milchkuh' ('Milk Cow') submarine tanker setting sail for the area at the end of that month.

But despite the reduced rate of losses since 1940, Joubert pointed out that unless the loss rate was reduced dramatically Britain could not survive more than a year. The stage was set for further battles with Bomber Command, who continued to regard the Battle of the Atlantic as an irrelevant side-show.

Joubert demanded the immediate transfer of six Wellington squadrons from Bomber Command, with a longer term provision of 81 Fortresses or Liberators. With a new AOC-in-C Bomber Command (Arthur Harris) appointed at this time, the transfers did not occur at once, and Coastal Command initially received only a trickle of obsolete Whitleys. More and more weight was shouldered by the remaining Sunderlands, which had to replace three Catalina units (Nos 209, 240 and 413 Sqns) that had been sent overseas.

Coastal Command also came close to losing one of its precious Sunderland units following Japan's entry into the war, for Australia requested the recall of No 10 Sqn RAAF – legally only 'on loan' to the RAF – to counter the Japanese navy threat. Fortunately, a deal was worked out whereby the squadron, with its hard-won experience, remained in the theatre it knew so well, and Catalinas on order for the RAF were transferred to the RAAF, where their longer range and improved hot-and-high performance and reliability proved even more useful.

In fact with production finally getting into its stride, and with the Empire Training Scheme getting into its stride, 1942 would see the formation of no less than five new UK-based Sunderland units. Shorts and Blackburn would produce 114 flying boats during 1942, a figure which outstripped the year's losses (24 UK-based aircraft), and which produced a small surplus to equip the new units. The first of these was the Australian-manned No 461 Sqn, formed from a cadre provided by No 10 Sqn RAAF, which stood up at Mount Batten on 25 April. Declared Operational (with six aircraft on charge) on 1 July, the unit had eleven aircraft by the end of the month.

Next to form was No 423 Sqn RCAF at Oban on 18 May, and it commenced operations on 23 August. At Bowmore, No 246 Sqn formed on 1 September, becoming operational on 12 December. This latter unit was destined to enjoy only a short association with the Sunderland, for it disbanded on 30 April 1943. The fourth unit to receive Sunderlands was No 119 Sqn at Bowmore, which had been formed on 13 March with a variety of flying boats. It had soon been declared non-operational, however, being employed principally in ferrying Catalinas from the USA. It was reassembled and transitioned onto Sunderland in September 1942 at Pembroke Dock, but would enjoy only a short life, for the unit disbanded there on 17 April 1943.

A second RCAF unit, No 422 Sqn, was destined to enjoy a much longer association with Coastal Command, forming with Lerwicks and Catalinas at Lough Erne on 2 April, and moving to Oban on 5 November. Here, it re-equipped with Sunderlands, becoming fully operational on 1 March 1943.

The existing units, meanwhile, were extremely busy, with the action in the Bay of Biscay in particular coming thick and fast. On 5 April 1942 two No 10 Sqn RAAF aircraft (W3994/X and W4004/Z) were tasked with covering the withdrawal of a commando force whose planned landing near Biarritz had been aborted in the face of severe weather. The aircraft remained on station for four hours, beating off no less than 14 attacks by Ju 88s. On 17 May, Flt Lt J G P Weatherlake of No 461 Sqn repelled repeated attacks by Ju 88s and limped back to base in what one

The original ASV radar installation included four aerial masts above the rear fuselage, Yagi antennas under the wingtips, and an antenna array on the sides of the rear fuselage. These are seen here on a Sunderland I of No 201 Sqn, photographed over a choppy Atlantic Ocean on 28 October 1941 (via Andy Thomas)

The view aft to the Sunderland's tail turret, illustrating the relatively roomy interior of the flying boat *(via Phil Jarrett)*

observer described as a 'Colander, perforated with about 200 20 mm cannon strikes!' On 27 July, Flt Lt R C W Humble of No 10 Sqn RAAF fought an hour-long battle with four Ju 88s, limping back to base with a damaged engine.

The following day another of the unit's aircraft, captained by Flt Lt Reg Marks, downed an attacking Bf 109 before being hit by flak, which damaged two engines. The RAAF pilot regained his base only by jettisoning all loose items, including the crew's parachutes. Fighters would continue to pose a hazard over the Bay of Biscay until August 1944, when Luftwaffe bases in northern France were abandoned in the face of the Allied advance, but by that time French U-Boat bases were also being deserted.

At last the Sunderland also began to share in the destruction of the still-elusive U-Boats. On 5 June 1942 W3986/U of No 10 Sqn RAAF damaged the Type VIIC vessel U-71, depth charging it as it dived and forcing the submarine to the surface, where it strafed it. The U-Boat fired back and damaged its assailant, before limping back to base submerged.

The Sunderland then came under attack by an Fw 200, which sat off outside machine gun range and sprayed the flying boat with cannon fire. Flt Lt S R C Wood and his crew kept their nerve, however, and fired back when the Fw 200 finally closed in at the end of the 75-minute running fight, finally driving it away with one German crew member dead and another wounded. On 7 June two more No 10 Sqn RAAF Sunderlands (W3994/X, flown by Plt Off T A Egerton and W4019/X, with Flt Lt E Yeoman at the controls) damaged the Italian submarine *Luigi Torello*, which had been successfully engaged two days earlier by a No 172 Sqn Wellington, and which was running for port on the surface with damaged steering gear. The Italian crew put up a spirited defence, causing casualties on both attacking aircraft, before seeking the safety of Spanish waters.

On 11 June 1942 Flt Lt Eric Martin of No 10 Sqn RAAF (in W3993/W) attacked the surfaced Type IXB U-105, damaging it badly enough to force it into the neutral Spanish port of El Ferrol. Two days later, a scratch Australian crew under the command of Sqn Ldr Burrage attacked the submarine *Otaria* while ferrying W4028/B out to join its new owners, No 228 Sqn!

As if to prove the inadequacy of the Sunderland's defensive armament, No 10 Sqn's W3999/Y was forced to alight after an attack by a single Arado Ar 196 floatplane. A nearby Whitley watched the

A rack of four 250-lb AS bombs is winched outboard from the fuselage of a Sunderland *(via Phil Jarrett)*

incident, and its crew were horrified to see the aircraft's starboard inner engine explode, sinking the Sunderland and leaving no survivors.

June 1942 saw Allied shipping construction figures overtake losses for the first time. Without a major increase in effectiveness, the U-Boats would henceforth be delaying the build up of the British and American merchant fleets, rather than actually reducing the overall tonnage. Experienced sailors were less easy to replace, of course, and there was some comfort for the Germans in the thought that only 50 per cent of the torpedoes fired actually hit their targets, the rest malfunctioning. If torpedo effectiveness could be improved, British losses would increase markedly.

Moreover, 1942 as a whole saw the U-Boats' kill-to-loss rate improve over that of the previous year, with more tonnage sunk for proportionally fewer losses. Sunderlands equipped with the improved ASV Mk II radar finally began reaching the frontline in June, however, and some guessed that the tide of the Battle was about to turn decisively in the Allies favour.

That month also saw the real debut of the Leigh Light on RAF Wellingtons, removing, at a stroke, the U-Boat's sanctuary of darkness. The impact of the Leigh light-equipped Wellingtons on U-Boat operations, in addition to the other factors, was immediate, and on 24 June Admiral Dönitz ordered his captains to proceed across the bay of Biscay submerged except when charging batteries, imposing a longer and more morale-sapping start and end to every patrol.

By this time Dönitz was again concentrating his submarines in the mid-Atlantic, where No 120 Sqn's handful of Liberators could stay on station for only a brief interval, and where no other land-based RAF aircraft could venture at all.

On 11 July 1942, Flt Lt Eddie Yeoman (the skipper of one of the Sunderlands which had attacked the *Luigi Torello* on 6 June), flying W4019/A of No 10 Sqn RAAF, attacked and damaged the U-162. Unfortunately, he would be posted missing in action four weeks later. Another No 10 Sqn casualty was Flt Lt Martin, whose crew went missing during a 30 July anti-shipping patrol off Spain – his aircraft was probably downed by a prowling Luftwaffe fighter. No 201 Sqn lost an aircraft on 31 July (to 'friendly' AA fire from Convoy WS 21), and a second (covering the same convoy) force-landed and exploded on 1 August.

August was a bad month for accidents, these accounting for two aircraft, one a No 4 OTU aircraft which crashed on landing at Invergordon, and the second being W4026 of No 228 Sqn, which hit high ground en route from Invergordon to Iceland. The rear-gunner miraculously survived, but the rest of the crew, and VIP passenger, HRH the Duke of Kent, perished.

Taken in May 1941, this official photograph well illustrates the tail turret fitted to early Sunderlands. The shot was taken as the aircraft neared completion on the Short production line. The turret's armament of four 0.303 in (rifle-calibre) machine guns was completely inadequate to meet the threat posed by German cannon-armed fighters *(via Phil Jarrett)*

At the same time, carefully co-ordinated Wolf Pack attacks began to make more and more of an impact, while the September introduction of the Metox radar detector (with a range greater than that of ASV) allowed U-Boats to crash dive before they could be found, and the number of contacts and sightings began to diminish. The answer was a new radar operating on a different wavelength, but because the set selected, ASV Mk III, used some common components with the H2S bombing radar, its introduction was delayed while priority was given to meeting Bomber Command's requirements. In the event, ASV Mk III did not appear on frontline Sqns until the beginning of 1943.

The Sunderland's pitifully under-armed nose turret could be retracted aft to leave a mooring compartment in front of it. The massive proportions of the aircraft may be discerned by the size of the figure in the cockpit (via Phil Jarrett)

No 461 Sqn's Flg Off H H Hosband (in T9113/B) was shot down over the Bay of Biscay on 1 September, probably by Ju 88Cs from 5/KG 40 which operated from Kerlin Bastard and Merignac. These were armed with a battery of three nose-mounted 20 mm cannon, and generally hunted in twos and threes, specialising in making simultaneous attacks from several directions. On the same day another of No 461 Sqn's aircraft joined with two from No 10 Sqn RAAF in an attack on the Italian submarine *Reginaldo Guiliano* The two No 10 Sqn aircraft (W3986/U, and W3983/R) were flown by Flt Lts Wood and Pockley, who dropped 250-lb semi-AP bombs and strafed the submarine, killing the captain and some of the crew. The submarine was attacked the next day by a Wellington, but survived to limp into Santander for extensive repairs.

In the North Atlantic, the presence of escort aircraft tended to have a remarkable effect on reducing shipping losses, even when outbound convoys were picked up leaving US/Canadian waters. In December 1940, HX-217 left the mouth of the St Lawrence facing 30 U-Boats, but lost only two ships (the following convoy SC-111 lost none) while the Liberators and Catalinas accounted for two U-Boat sinkings from sixteen attacks. The two ships sunk were lost either before the close escort Liberator arrived on scene, or on the one day when poor weather prevented air operations altogether.

In December 1942 it was announced that Coastal Command's AOC-in-C (Sir Phillip Joubert) would be replaced by Sir John Slessor, who finally took up his post on 5 February 1943. Joubert had become quite unpopular due to his persistence in pressing for the anti-U-Boat war to be accorded a higher priority. And in a supreme stroke of irony, he was still in command during the Casablanca Conference, at which it was stated that British and US resources would finally be directed 'first and foremost' at the defeat of the U-Boat – just what he had been pressing for since his appointment. The bombing of the U-Boat pens (which he'd also urged) was finally approved, although these were now virtually bomb-proof thanks to the delay.

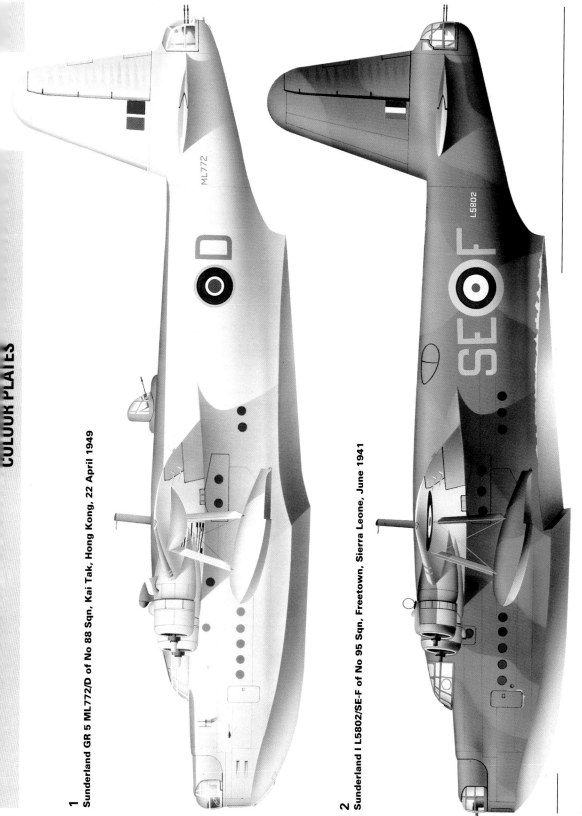

1
Sunderland GR 5 ML772/D of No 88 Sqn, Kai Tak, Hong Kong, 22 April 1949

2
Sunderland I L5802/SE-F of No 95 Sqn, Freetown, Sierra Leone, June 1941

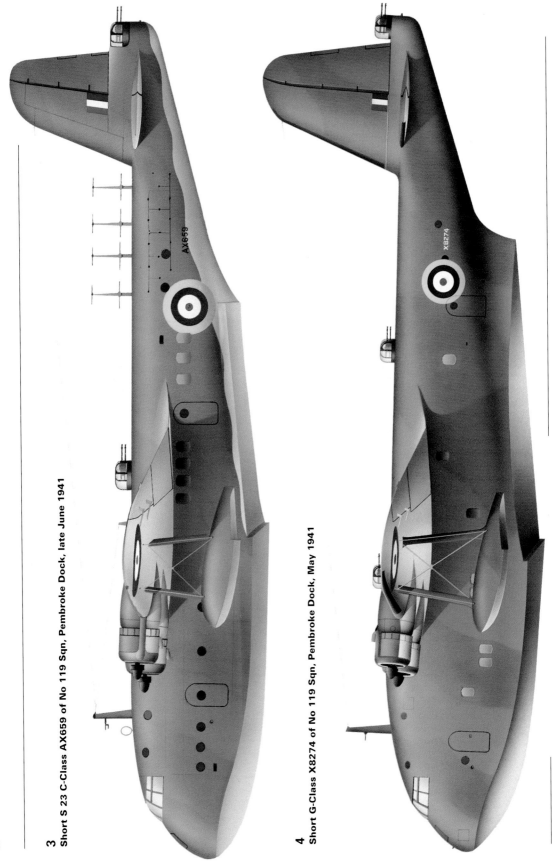

3
Short S 23 C-Class AX659 of No 119 Sqn, Pembroke Dock, late June 1941

4
Short G-Class X8274 of No 119 Sqn, Pembroke Dock, May 1941

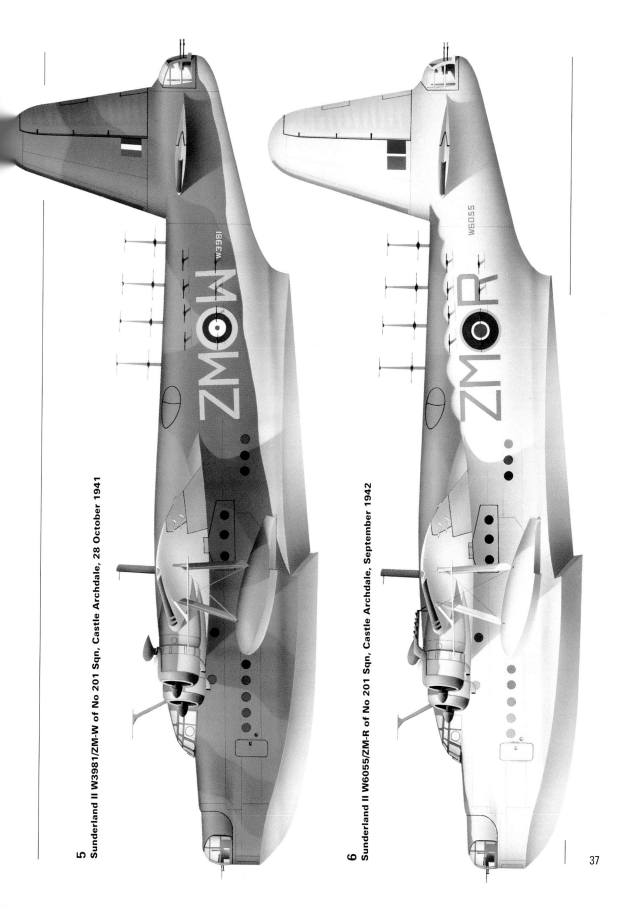

5
Sunderland II W3981/ZM-W of No 201 Sqn, Castle Archdale, 28 October 1941

6
Sunderland II W6055/ZM-R of No 201 Sqn, Castle Archdale, September 1942

37

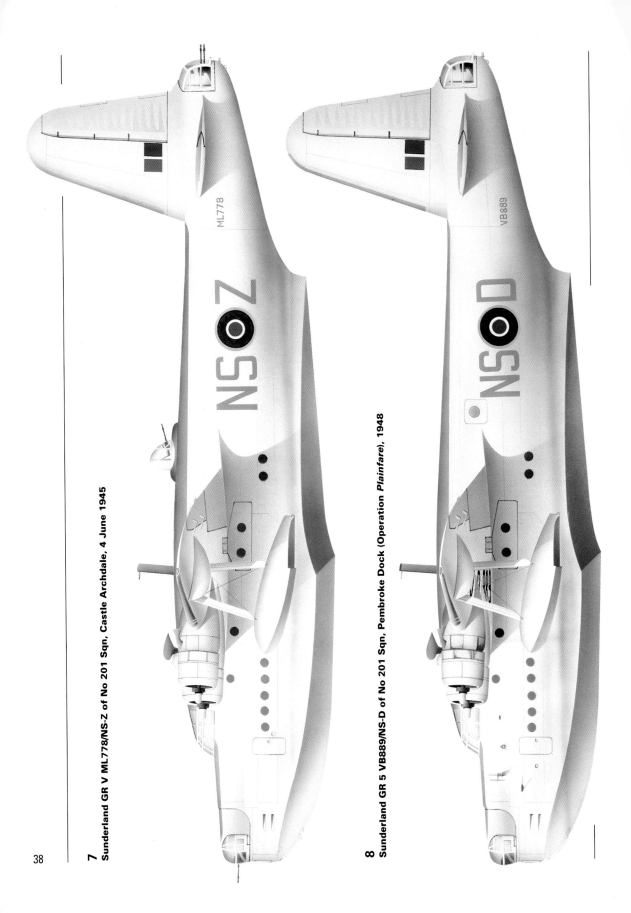

7
Sunderland GR V ML778/NS-Z of No 201 Sqn, Castle Archdale, 4 June 1945

8
Sunderland GR 5 VB889/NS-D of No 201 Sqn, Pembroke Dock (Operation *Plainfare*), 1948

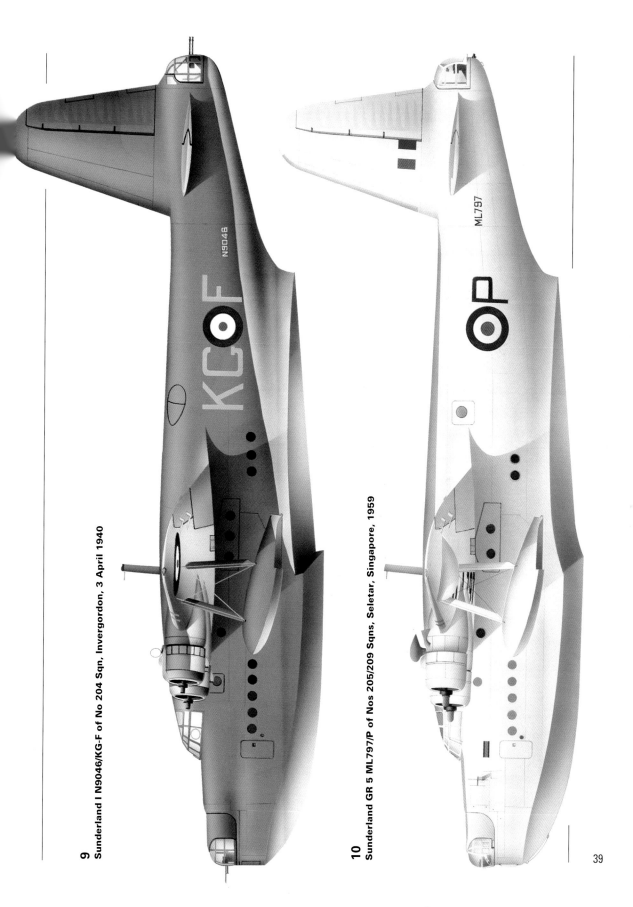

9

Sunderland I N9046/KG-F of No 204 Sqn, Invergordon, 3 April 1940

10

Sunderland GR 5 ML797/P of Nos 205/209 Sqns, Seletar, Singapore, 1959

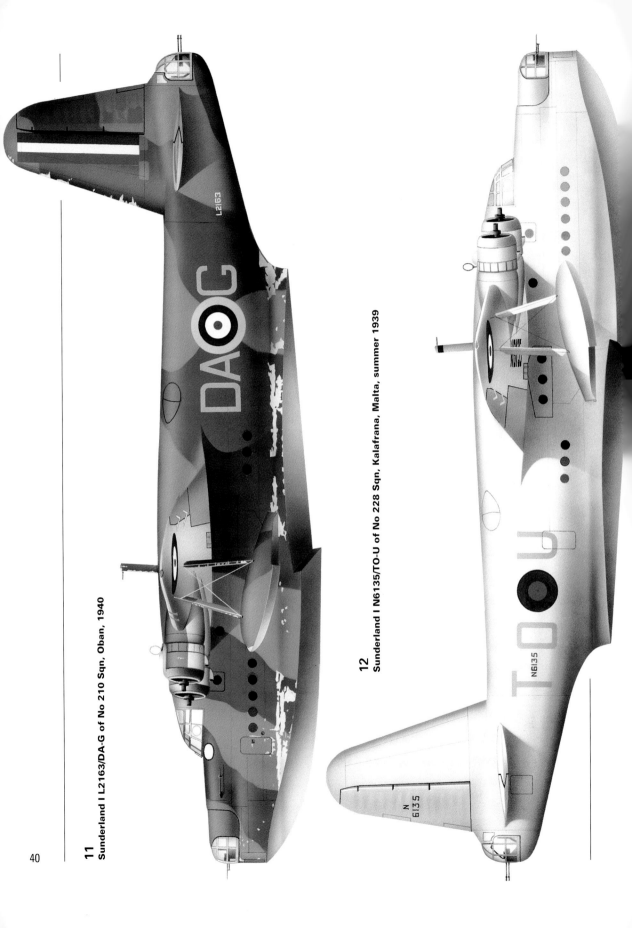

11
Sunderland I L2163/DA-G of No 210 Sqn, Oban, 1940

L2163

DA·G

12
Sunderland I N6135/TO-U of No 228 Sqn, Kalafrana, Malta, summer 1939

TO·U

N6135

N 6135

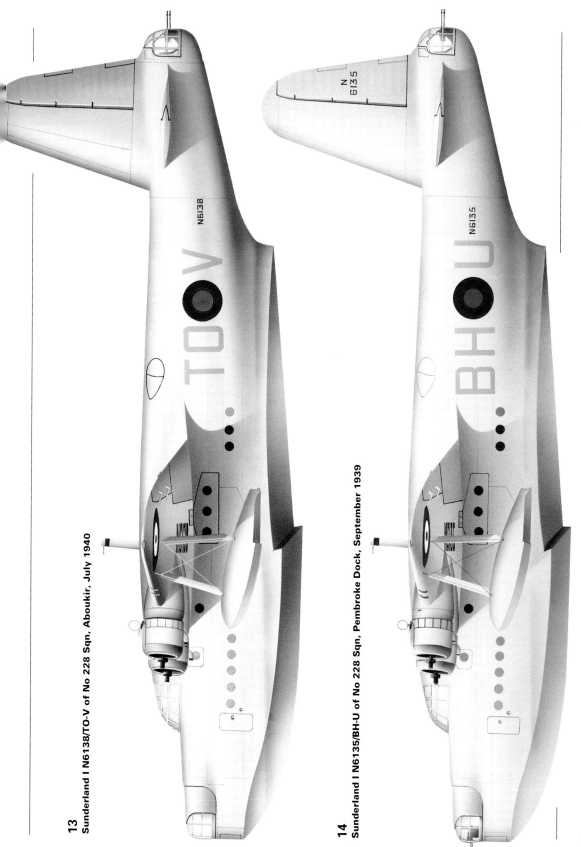

13
Sunderland I N6138/TO-V of No 228 Sqn, Aboukir, July 1940

14
Sunderland I N6135/BH-U of No 228 Sqn, Pembroke Dock, September 1939

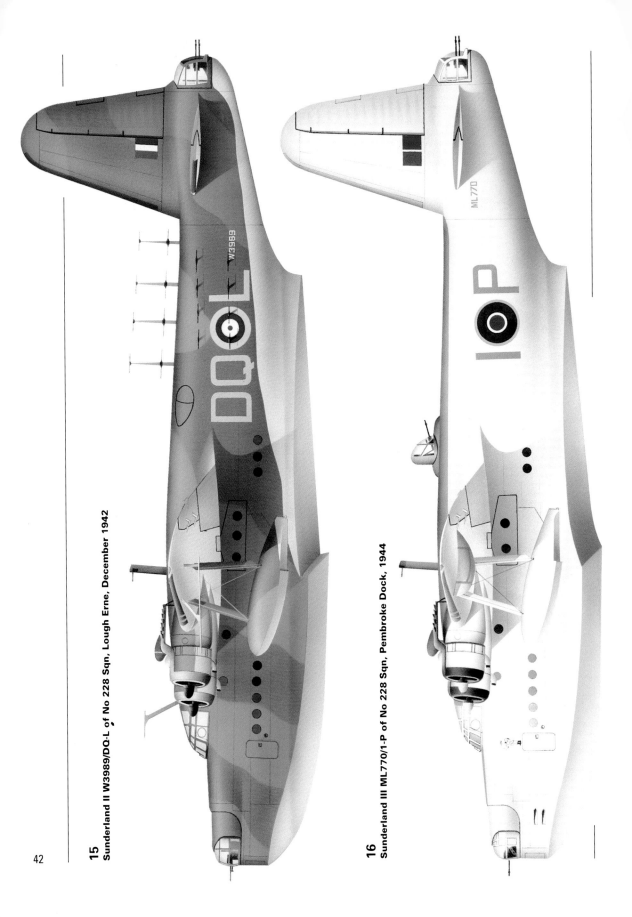

15
Sunderland II W3989/DQ-L of No 228 Sqn, Lough Erne, December 1942

16
Sunderland III ML770/1-P of No 228 Sqn, Pembroke Dock, 1944

17
Sunderland I L2160 *Selangor* of No 230 Sqn, Seletar, Singapore, October 1938

18
Sunderland I N9029/NM-V of the No 230 Sqn Detachment at Scaramanga, 1941

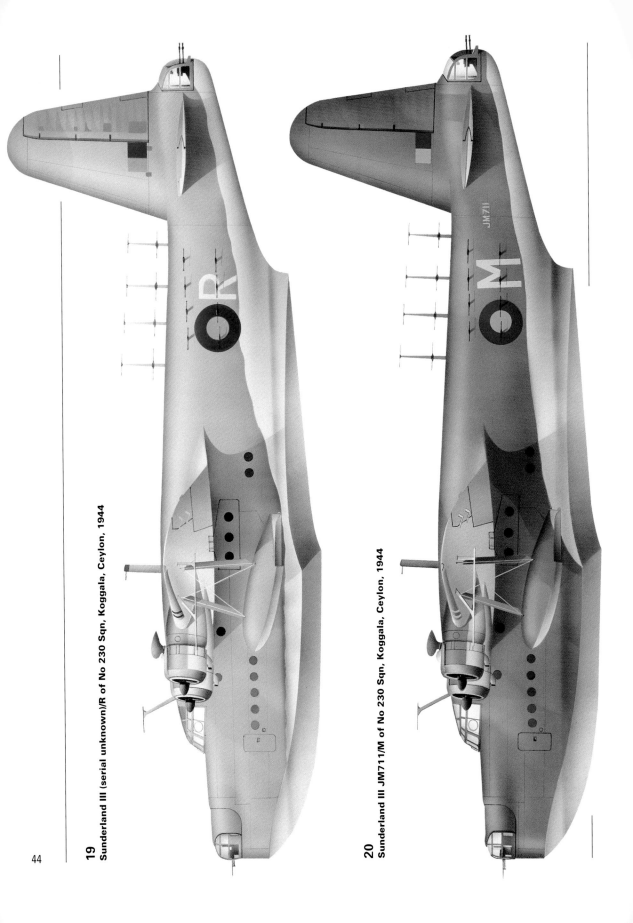

19
Sunderland III (serial unknown)/R of No 230 Sqn, Koggala, Ceylon, 1944

20
Sunderland III JM711/M of No 230 Sqn, Koggala, Ceylon, 1944

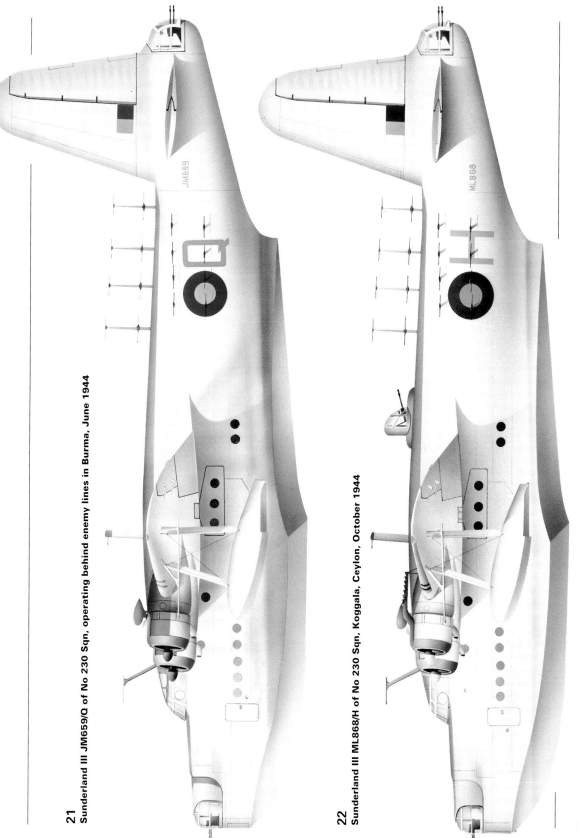

21
Sunderland III JM659/Q of No 230 Sqn, operating behind enemy lines in Burma, June 1944

22
Sunderland III ML868/H of No 230 Sqn, Koggala, Ceylon, October 1944

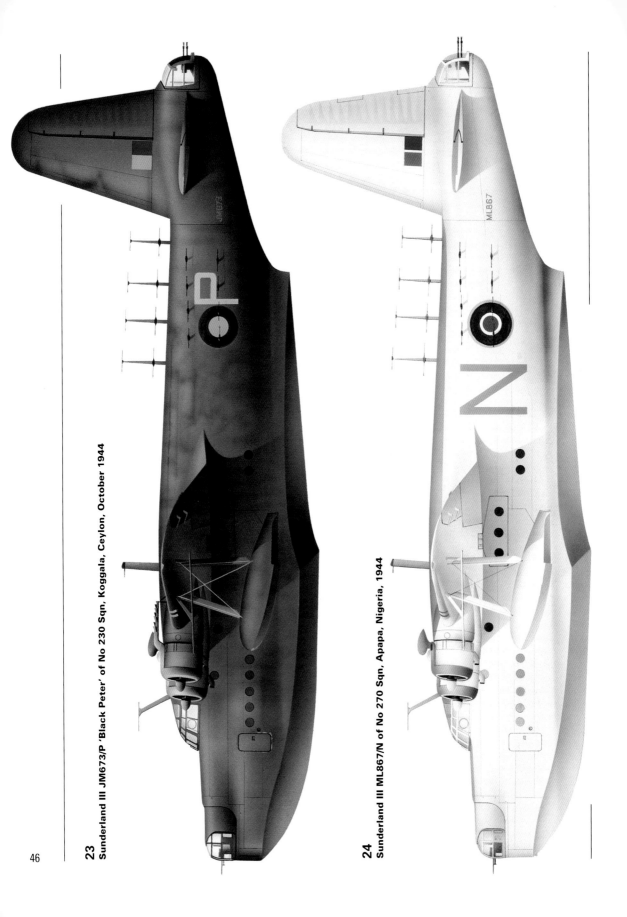

23
Sunderland III JM673/P 'Black Peter' of No 230 Sqn, Koggala, Ceylon, October 1944

24
Sunderland III ML867/N of No 270 Sqn, Apapa, Nigeria, 1944

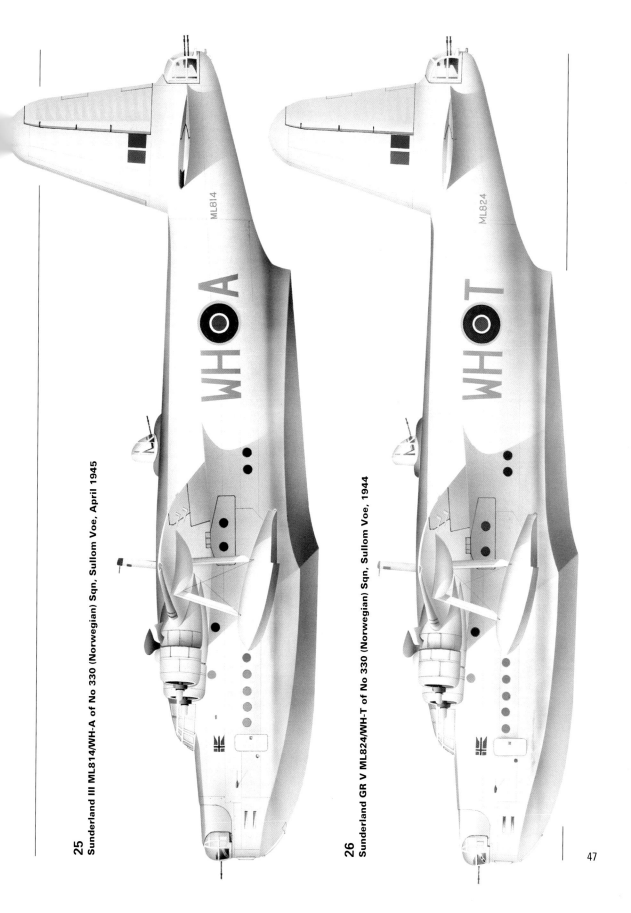

25
Sunderland III ML814/WH-A of No 330 (Norwegian) Sqn, Sullom Voe, April 1945

26
Sunderland GR V ML824/WH-T of No 330 (Norwegian) Sqn, Sullom Voe, 1944

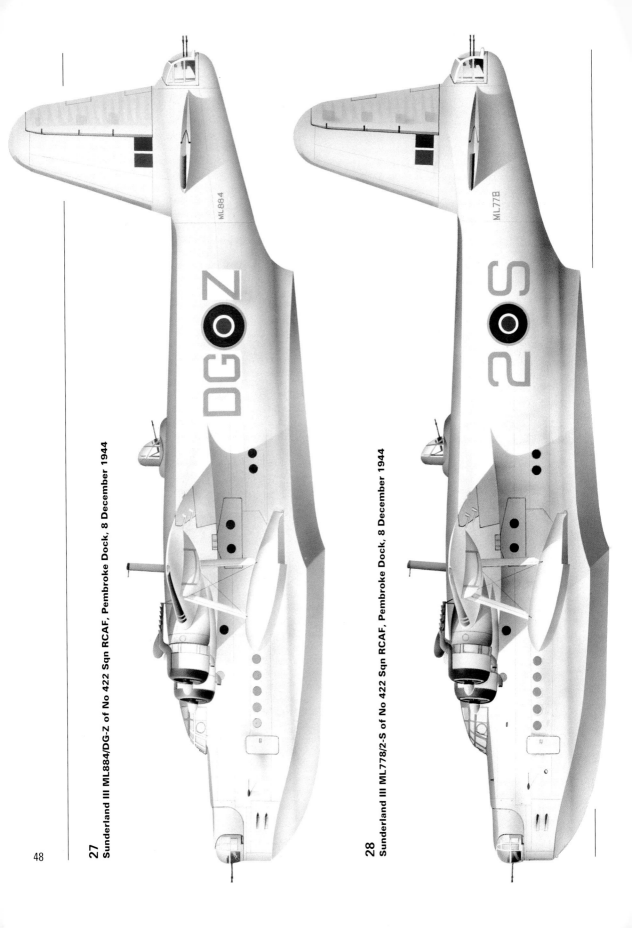

27
Sunderland III ML884/DG-Z of No 422 Sqn RCAF, Pembroke Dock, 8 December 1944

28
Sunderland III ML778/2-S of No 422 Sqn RCAF, Pembroke Dock, 8 December 1944

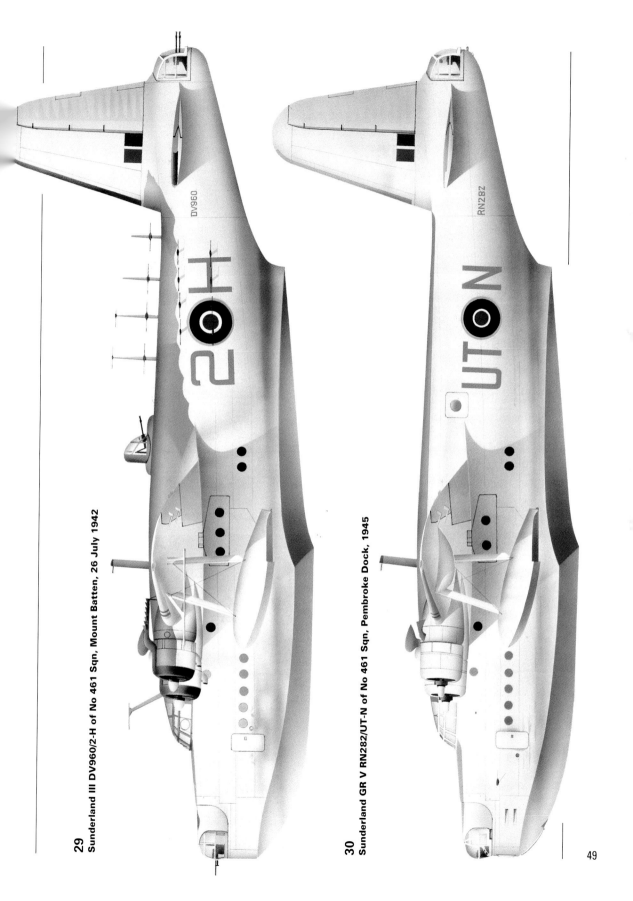

29
Sunderland III DV960/2-H of No 461 Sqn, Mount Batten, 26 July 1942

30
Sunderland GR V RN282/UT-N of No 461 Sqn, Pembroke Dock, 1945

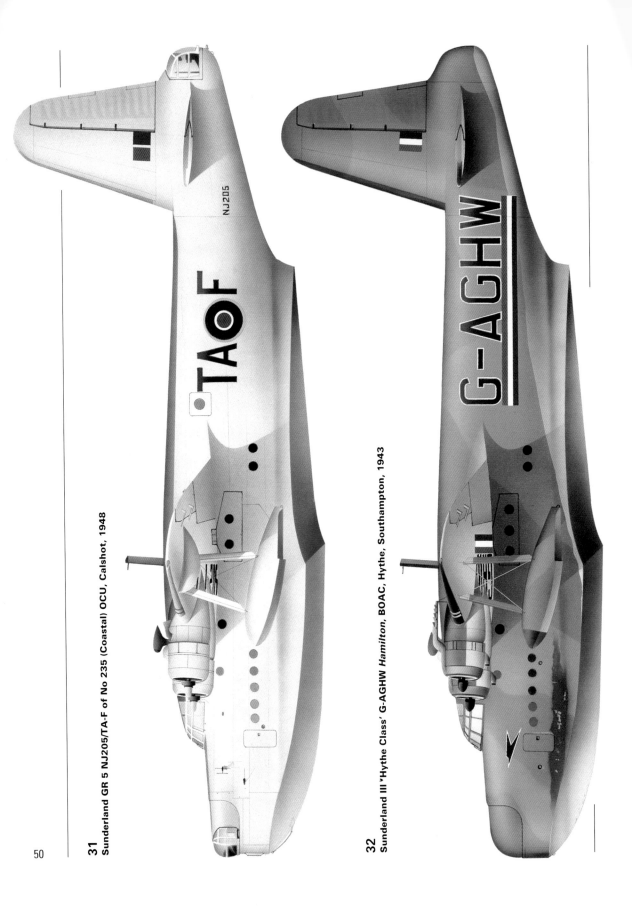

31
Sunderland GR 5 NJ205/TA-F of No 235 (Coastal) OCU, Calshot, 1948

32
Sunderland III 'Hythe Class' G-AGHW *Hamilton*, BOAC, Hythe, Southampton, 1943

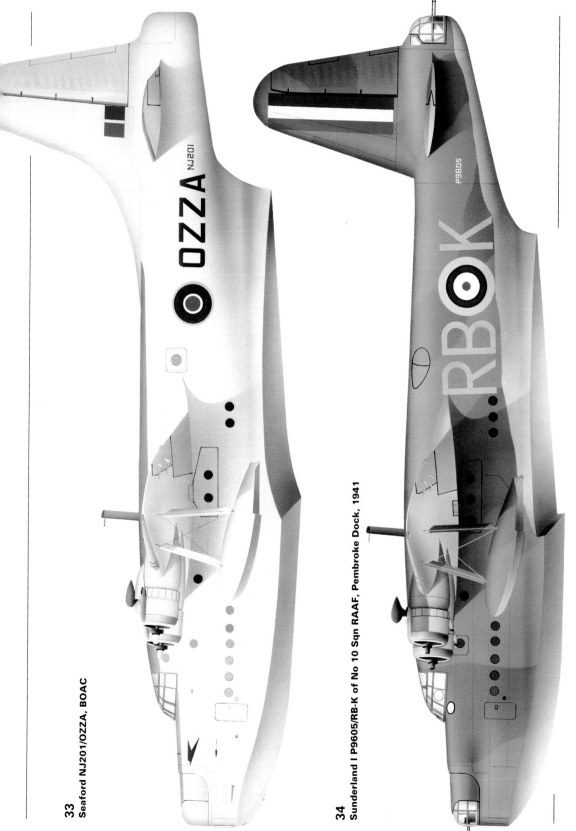

33
Seaford NJ201/OZZA, BOAC

34
Sunderland I P9605/RB-K of No 10 Sqn RAAF, Pembroke Dock, 1941

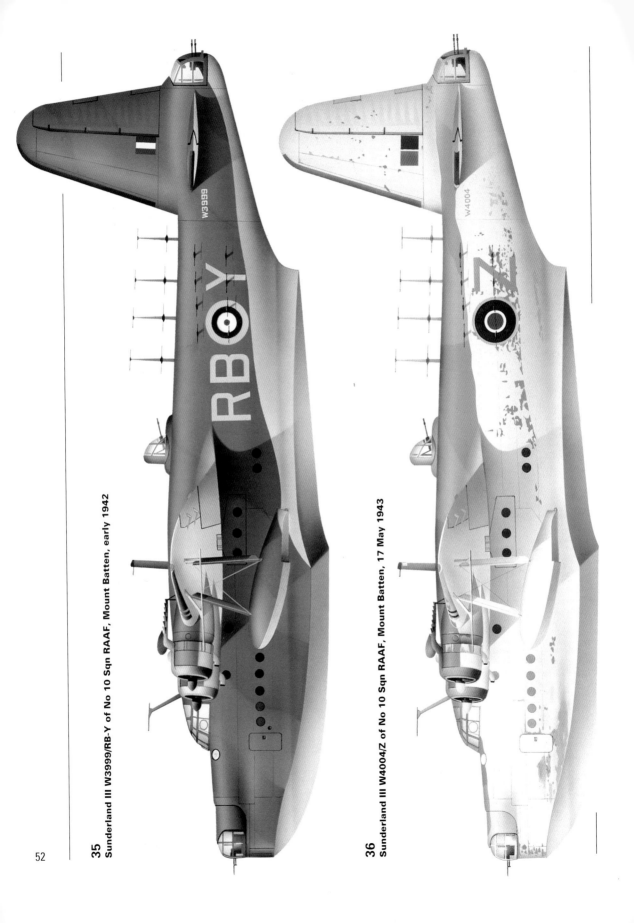

35
Sunderland III W3999/RB-Y of No 10 Sqn RAAF, Mount Batten, early 1942

36
Sunderland III W4004/Z of No 10 Sqn RAAF, Mount Batten, 17 May 1943

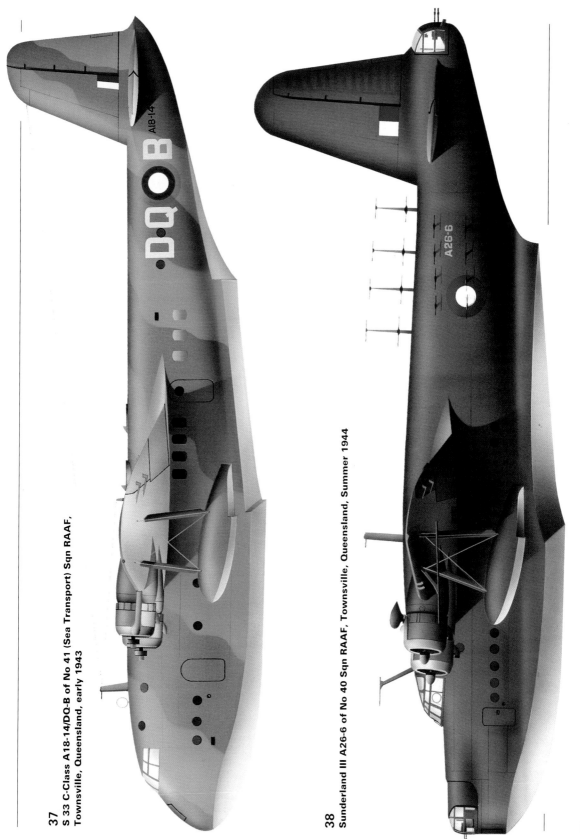

37
S 33 C-Class A18-14/DQ-B of No 41 (Sea Transport) Sqn RAAF,
Townsville, Queensland, early 1943

38
Sunderland III A26-6 of No 40 Sqn RAAF, Townsville, Queensland, Summer 1944

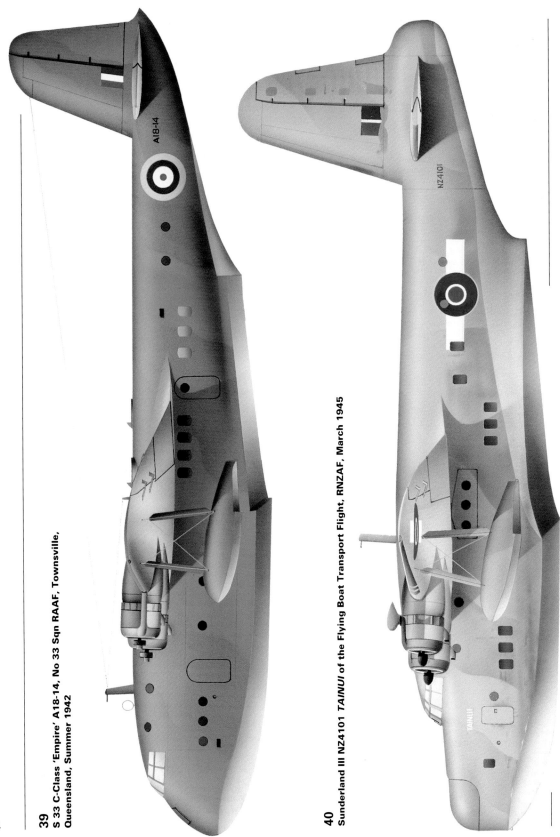

39
S 33 C-Class 'Empire' A18-14, No 33 Sqn RAAF, Townsville,
Queensland, Summer 1942

40
Sunderland III NZ4101 *TAINUI* of the Flying Boat Transport Flight, RNZAF, March 1945

WINNING THE BATTLE

When Sir John Slessor formally took over from Joubert as Coastal Command's new AOC-in-C on 5 February 1943, the RAF could field seven Sunderland units, and two more were forming. The day before he took command, on 4 February 1943, No 19 Group launched Operation *Gondola*. Intelligence reports had indicated that 45 U-Boats would transit through the Bay of Biscay between 3-13 February, so Coastal Command launched a 12-day effort to intensively patrol a rectangle of sea through which the vessels would have to pass. Sunderlands participated, but scored neither of the operation's two kills.

The use of 'Wolf Pack' tactics by Dönitz (soon to be C-in-C of the entire German navy, following the March sacking of Raeder) in early 1943 again threatened to impose an unsustainable rate of losses on Allied merchantmen. This loss rate was a great worry, and occurred despite the fact that Coastal Command successfully prevented many submarines from reaching their attack positions. Those which did slip through did massive damage however, and the sinking of U-Boats remained rare.

Unfortunately, there were simply still too few aircraft to provide the necessary cover, and while President Roosevelt personally intervened to unblock the flow of Liberators to Coastal Command (and the RCAF), the Royal Navy was unsuccessful in pressing their request for the transfer of 190 Lancasters from Bomber Command. Sunderland production, meanwhile, was insufficient to allow anything more than the slowest expansion of the force, and although production would total 202 aircraft in 1943, (the highest for any year) many went overseas, and the size of the UK-based Sunderland force remained virtually constant – it actually shrunk in size by one squadron during the early part of the year.

No 330 Sqn at Sullom Voe traded Catalinas for Sunderlands in February 1943, becoming operational on 20 April. But that same month saw the disbandment of two other UK-based Sunderland units, namely

The prototype Mk III (T9042) first flew on 28 June 1941, and was to prove the most successful and widely used of the wartime variants. This aircraft was photographed on 22 October 1943, by which time it had been passed on to No 4 OTU. The training unit had 23 Sunderland Mk IIs and 8 Mk IIIs on strength at this time, flying them from Alness (formerly Invergordon). This made it the largest single operator of the Shorts flying boat by some considerable margin. T9042 remained on strength with the OTU until struck off charge in February 1945 *(via Phil Jarrett)*

The principal difference between the Sunderland Mk II and the Mk III was the neatly faired main step, which reduced drag without degrading hydrodynamic characteristics *(via Phil Jarrett)*

By 1943 most Sunderlands were operating in a new colour scheme apparently modelled on that of the Herring Gull, featuring dark sea grey and green camouflaged topsides and white undersides. This No 422 Sqn Mk III (DD862) is seen off Iceland during May 1943, the Blackburn-built aircraft serving with the Canadian unit throughout its frontline career. The flying boat was finally lost at Castle Archdale on 31 May 1945 when it burnt out after landing with an engine on fire *(via Andy Thomas)*

Nos 119 and 246 Sqns. This, however, allowed the remaining units to finally get to an establishment of 12 aircraft each, instead of the nine which had become the norm. There were also a number of changes of name to some of the Sunderland bases, with Lough Erne reverting to Castle Archdale in January, and with Invergordon becoming Lanes on 10 February. No 461 Sqn had moved to BOAC's Poole base (known as Hamworthy Junction) in September 1942, flying night sorties from Mount Batten until it moved to Pembroke Dock in April 1943.

These changes left three units at Castle Archdale (Nos 201, 228 and 423), one at Pembroke Dock (No 461), one at Mount Batten (No 10 RAAF) and two at Oban (Nos 330 and 422).

March and April 1943 were marked by a series of kill claims by the Sunderlands. On 19 March 1943 DD837/V of No 228 Sqn attacked U-608 and claimed it as damaged. Better seemed to follow the following day, when Flg Off W C Robertson of No 201 Sqn (flying W6051/T) tried to attack a U-Boat which vanished below the waves as he arrived. Forty minutes later, however, he spotted a surfaced U-Boat about six miles away, and attacked it with depth charges. Coming under heavy fire from the submarine's machine guns and cannon, the crew reported seeing the U-Boat slide below the surface 'stern first' and the Sunderland was credited with the destruction of U-384.

Postwar research revealed that U-384 had actually been sunk the previous day (by a Fortress II of No 206 Sqn) and that Robertson had actually attacked U-631, and that he had failed to sink the submarine. On the same day, DD829/Z of No 202 Sqn attacked and damaged U-527.

The Royal Navy awarded another 'Sunk' assessment to Flt Lt C L Bradley of No 423 Sqn, who attacked U-338 in W6008/H on 5 April 1943. The submarine was actually only lightly damaged, although it was sunk five months later. Another U-Boat officially categorised as being sunk after an attack by Sunderlands was U-119, engaged on 29 April 1943 by Flg Offs R de V Gipps of No 461 Sqn (flying P) and N C Gerrard of No 10 Sqn RAAF (in DP177/F). But the Sunderlands' depth charges fell wide, and the submarine escaped damage, although it too would be sunk two months later.

But the run of apparent successes could not mask the fact that the battle was going badly for the Allies, and shipping losses were reaching an unsustainable level.

The war in the Atlantic did then begin to turn decisively against the U-Boat, most notably with the introduction of the aircraft-carried torpedo. This gave patrol aircraft

the ability to attack U-Boats underwater, and effectively removed the sanctuary of depth, and ensured that submarines could be attacked even if they submerged below periscope depth. Unfortunately, the Sunderland was unable to carry the weapon. However, they were by now routinely equipped with radar (often the Centimetric ASV Mk III), while Coastal Command and the Royal Navy continued to receive invaluable intelligence from *Ultra*.

At his Paris HQ, Dönitz was convinced that the German naval ciphers had been broken (as was his intelligence chief, Vice Admiral Erhard Maertens), but his cryptographers assured him that Enigma was 'uncrackable'! As a result of these advances, 41 U-Boats were sunk during May 1943 (23 by aircraft, and at least five by Sunderlands) and on 22 May Dönitz redeployed his Wolf Packs to the Azores, South America and the Caribbean, giving the hard-pressed Atlantic convoys brief respite.

On 1 May 1943, Flt Lt E C Smith of No 461 Sqn, flying DV698/M, found and attacked U-415 (a Type VIIC) damaged earlier in the day by a Leigh Light Wellington. The U-Boat submerged, damaged further, and despite being set upon six hours later by a Whitley, limped back to Brest. Flt Lt Smith (flying the same aircraft) had more success the following day, dropping eight depth charges on U-332 (a Type VIIC) which went down by the stern and sank, at least 15 of its crew jumping for it before the submarine slipped stern first beneath the waves. In both cases, the U-Boats remained on the surface and attempted to fight back – a worrying new development for aircrew, but one which left their targets vulnerable on the surface for longer. While the anti-aircraft armament fitted to the sub-marines remained light, the balance probably lay in the aircraft's favour.

But targets which fought back were not the only hazard facing the RAF aircrew, especially in the Bay of Biscay, where heavily-armed Ju 88s of V./KG 40 roamed in packs of six or eight searching for solitary Liberators or Sunderlands. Despite morale-boosting extra armament fitted by some units (most notably No 10 Sqn RAAF), usually the only chance of survival was to reach the sanctuary of cloud.

On 2 June 1943, Flt Lt J C Walker of No 461 Sqn defied the odds and managed to fight off an attack by eight Ju 88s, his gunners downing three of the attackers and driving off another. But the Sunderland was badly damaged, with one crewman dead and others wounded. On returning, Walker beached his aircraft near Penzance

Well-worn Mk III DV960 was serving with No 461 Sqn when it was photographed on patrol over the Western Approaches on 26 July 1943. Part of a batch of 25 Mk IIIs built by Shorts at Rochester between June and October 1942, this aircraft spent its entire frontline career with the Australian-manned unit. DV960 was eventually passed on to No 131 (Coastal) OTU at Killadeas, just south of Castle Archdale, where it joined 18 other Sunderlands and no fewer than 28 Catalinas. The veteran flying boat was eventually struck off charge on 31 May 1945 (via Andy Thomas)

This Mk III (DP191) was photographed at anchor at Castle Archdale in 1943 while serving with the largely Canadian-manned No 423 Sqn. It survived the war and, as a Mk 5, served with the RNZAF as NZ4109 into the 1960s (via Andy Thomas)

No 461 Sqn's T9114/E is seen under tow behind the French sloop *La Combattante* on 29 May 1943 in the Bay of Biscay. Hours later, in heavier seas, the tow rope parted and Plt Off Singleton was forced to take off in the aircraft to avoid it being sunk. A hole was ripped in its side during the take off, and the pilot elected to land on the grass beside the concrete runway at Angle, near Pembroke Dock. It never flew again, being subsequently redesignated a maintenance airframe
(via Andy Thomas)

Beached! Sunderland II W6058 of the short-lived No 246 Sqn broke free from its moorings at Bowmore, on the island of Islay, in Strathclyde, during a gale in early 1943 and was blown ashore. The aircraft was undamaged, and went on to enjoy a long career. Interestingly, the original print was heavily (and quite subtly) censored, leaving little trace of the ASV radar fit
(via Bruce Robertson)

to prevent it sinking. He was subsequently awarded a DSO, and his crewmen a DFC and two DFMs. Most of them were subsequently killed on 13 August, when six Ju 88s shot down DV968 over the Bay of Biscay.

But U-Boat kills continued to mount up. On 7 May Flt Lt G G Rossiter (flying W3993/W) of No 10 Sqn RAAF attacked a submarine with eight depth charges, leaving the vessel circling unsteadily and trailing oil, before slowly submerging about half an hour later. The U-465, another Type VIIC, was lost with all hands in the same location at the same time, and is assumed to have been Rossiter's victim. On 13 May W6006/3-G of No 423 Sqn (flown by Flt Lt J Musgrave), attacked the Type VIIC U-Boat U-456 (which had already been damaged by a Liberator the previous day), as it tried to submerge in the mid Atlantic. The submarine was subsequently finished off by a frigate and a corvette.

On 17 May Rossiter found another U-Boat, forcing it to crash dive three times in the space of an hour, before being forced to return to base. While Rossiter played 'cat-and-mouse' with the U-Boat, his fellow Aussie, No 461 Sqn's Flt Lt J G P Weatherlake had to fight off six Ju 88s, while on the same day, Flt Lt K McKenzie of No 10 Sqn RAAF failed to return, having been shot down by a gaggle of Junkers heavy fighters.

A Sunderland of No 228 Sqn (EJ139/L), flown by Flt Lt H J Debnam, bit off more than it could chew on 24 May 1943 when it attacked the Type VIIC U-441. This was no ordinary Type VIIC, however, since it served as an experimental prototype for the *Unterseebootfleugzeugfalle* (U-Boat aircraft trap), with 16 extra crew embarked (all experienced gunners) to man two four-barrelled 20 mm cannon and a 37 mm anti-aircraft gun. The Sunderland was badly damaged, and was easy meat for the Ju 88s which then attacked it. The only consolation was that one of the U-441's new 'bandstands' was giving trouble, and without all of its guns firing, the

Another censored picture shows Sunderland II W3991 of No 228 Sqn beached at Pembroke Dock during August 1943 while new hardstandings were being prepared. The aircraft's well-worn topsides are clearly evident. W3991 was passed on to No 3 Flying Boat Servicing Unit – also at Pembroke Dock – in November 1943, and was finally recatagorised Instructional Airframe 5016M in early 1945 *(via Bruce Robertson)*

submarine did absorb some damage. On its next patrol U-441 was set upon by three Beaufighters, which killed or wounded most of the deck crew and almost sank the vessel, which limped back to its base.

Four days later No 461 Sqn lost another Sunderland. Flt Lt W S E Dodds found the crew of a ditched Whitley and gained permission to land and pick them up. Unfortunately, he bounced off the waves three times and then stalled. Dodds was killed, the aircraft broke up and the rest of the crew took to their dinghy. Another No 461 Sqn Sunderland, piloted by Plt Off G O Singleton, landed alongside and took the survivors aboard, but could not take off with the extra weight. Singleton's aircraft was then taken on tow by a Free French sloop, which took off the survivors and all but four of Singleton's crew. The tow rope parted four hours later, and Singleton managed to take off, although the heavy seas ripped a seven-foot gash in the aircraft's hull. On return to base, Singleton landed on the grass at Angle airfield – a first for the Sunderland.

Two U-Boats were sunk by Sunderlands on the last day of the month. After 18 months on No 201 Sqn, Flt Lt Douglas Gall had never seen a U-Boat, and expected his patrol in DD835/R to be what he called '15 hours of watching water – utter boredom'. Almost seven hours into the patrol he sighted a Type VIIC U-Boat fully surfaced eight miles off to starboard. The U-Boat stayed on the surface as Gall dived in to the attack, with the U-Boat gunners and Plt Off Martin in the Sunderland's nose turret trading fire. Gall's depth charges were falling well awry, but U-440 turned rapidly right into the middle of the stick and was sunk. The next victim was U-563 (another Type VIIC), which had been found and attacked by a pair of Halifaxes before being further damaged by Flt Lt Max Mainprize of No 10 Sqn RAAF in DV969/E. Finally, Flg Off W M

French of No 228 Sqn (in DD838/X) made another attack, which literally blew the U-Boat apart. The sea was left littered with wreckage and survivors, and one of the Halifaxes flew low over the scene, dropping its dinghies and Mae Wests to the bemused Germans.

Having ordered his U-Boats from the mid-Atlantic to its peripheries, Dönitz further directed his commanders to stay submerged by night, and to surface only to recharge their batteries. He also directed them to move in groups, entering and leaving port only in the early morning or late evening, and only when the approaches were covered by the Luftwaffe. The changes worked in the short term, and in early June, U-Boat sightings were few and far between. But later in the month, Coastal Command became aware of the changes, and sunk five and damaged eight U-Boats. Sunderlands were responsible for damaging two U-Boats during June.

On 13 June No 228 Sqn's Flg Off Lee, captain of DV967/U, sighted a group of five U-Boats north of Cape Ortegal and attacked and badly damaged the Type VIIC U-564, before being shot down by accurate and heavy return fire from several submarines. The damaged submarine, escorted by U-185, set course for Brest and survived an attack by a Whitley (which was in turn damaged by the U-Boat and then downed by fighters).

On 27 June Flg Off B E H Layne of No 201 Sqn, skipper of W6005/P, attacked and damaged Type IXC submarine U-518, forcing it to submerge after a prolonged gunnery duel, after which the U-Boat returned to Lorient for repairs. On 12 July No 228 Sqn lost DV977 (captained by Sgt Codd) to the ever-present Ju 88s, but the unit took its revenge the following day when Flg Off D R Hanbury (flying JM708/N) attacked a trio of U-Boats with gunfire, making a depth charge attack when one (U-607, a Type VIIC) strayed. The bows and conning tower were blown off and the U-Boat sank immediately. Hanbury circled and dropped a dinghy for the survivors.

The absence of squadron badges made Sunderland units difficult to identify, especially when two-letter codes were not carried, or when they were replaced by station-based numerical codes. This aircraft, (DD851), however, was pictured at Sullom Voe in 1943 while serving with the Norwegian-manned No 330 Sqn. Part of a batch of 40 Mk IIIs built by Blackburn Aircraft in Dumbarton between December 1942 and June 1943, DD851 was issued to No 330 Sqn just as the unit was re-equipping with Sunderlands. One of five Mk IIIs delivered to the Norwegian unit 'fresh from the factory', it was eventually passed on to No 4 (Coastal) OTU. DD851 was written off whilst still serving with the Alness-based training unit when it crashed near Invergordon on 26 November 1944 (via Andy Thomas)

This Sunderland III (ML740/E of No 461 Sqn, captained by Flg Off Bunce) was shot down into the Bay of Biscay by nine Ju 88s on 23 May 1944, with the loss of five of its twelve crew (via Andy Thomas)

On 30 July 1943, a Sunderland from No 461 Sqn participated in the first combined air/sea operation against a group of three U-Boats. This trio had been sighted by a No 53 Sqn Liberator. A motley collection of aircraft (the Liberator was joined by a No 228 Sqn Sunderland, a No 210 Sqn Catalina, a USAAF B-24 and a No 502 Sqn Halifax) circled the U-Boats while surface vessels raced to the scene. The Halifax attacked first, followed by another, before the original No 53 Sqn

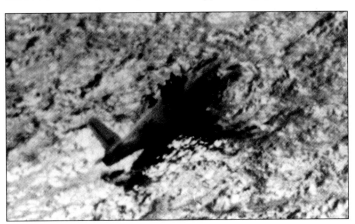

Liberator tipped in. This was badly damaged by flak, and had to force-land in Portugal. While the U-Boat gunners were distracted by the Liberator and Halifaxes, Flt Lt Dudley Marrows of No 461 Sqn (in W6077/U) attacked the Type XIV U-Boat U-461 at wave-top height, straddling it with seven Depth Charges. The U-Boat split in two and sank, and Marrows dropped a dinghy to the survivors. Sister-ship U-462 was sunk by the Halifaxes, and the third submarine, U-504, was then hunted and destroyed by the mixed bag of ships and aircraft. En route home, Marrows used his one remaining depth charge against another U-Boat, which his crew also machine-gunned. The U-Boat put up a hail of defensive fire, and Marrows turned for the Scillies, too low on fuel to reach his base.

Sunderlands continued their run of success into August, accounting for four of the five U-Boats sunk during the first four days of that month – other was claimed by a No 415 Sqn Hampden and a USAAF Liberator. But these engagements were not without cost. Dönitz's 'fight back' campaign officially ended on 2 August, and although 12 aircraft had been shot down since it began on 27 April, 26 U-Boats had been sunk and 17 more had been damaged.

The first few days of August were in many ways typical of this part of the campaign. For example, on the 1st, Flt Lt Bob Fry's W4020/B of No 10 Sqn RAAF was badly damaged while attacking the Type VIIC U-454. Attempting to force-land, the Sunderland broke up, and only six of the crew were rescued by the RN ship which raced to the scene, along with some survivors from the U-Boat.

Hours later, Flt Lt Stan White (flying JM678/V of No 228 Sqn) successfully attacked U-383 (a Type VIIC), which shot away his starboard float and aileron and holed the hull and port wing. The U-Boat was still afloat when White left the scene, but it foundered during the night, with the loss of its entire crew.

The next day the Type IXB U-106, en route home for repairs following an attack by a Wellington, was engaged by two Sunderlands. These were flown by Flt Lt R D Hanbury (JM708/N of No 228 Sqn) and Flg Off I A F 'Chick' Clark (DV698/M of No 461 Sqn), who attacked from opposite beams dropping their depth charges within a time-span of only 30 seconds. The U-Boat filled with smoke and chlorine, and the crew abandoned ship before it blew up and sank.

No 422 Sqn Sunderland III EK591 was the aircraft used by WO W F Morton and his crew to sink U-625 on 10 March 1944. It is seen here recovering at Castle Archdale on 15 July. Used exclusively in the frontline by the Canadian-manned unit, this aircraft eventually wound up at No 4 (Coastal) OTU and was finally struck off charge on 2 November 1945 (via Andy Thomas)

On 3 August Flg Off Alan Williams of No 10 Sqn RAAF came under attack from seven Ju 88s, and his aircraft was heavily damaged in the 80-minute combat which left one crewman dead and four more wounded. While Williams manoeuvred DD852/J as energetically as he could, the first fitter, Sgt W C Moser, crawled inside the wing to try and plug the ruptured fuel tank. The crew shared two DFCs and two DFMs.

On 4 August 1943 U-489 (a Type XIV *Milchkuh*) was lost, although it shot down its attacker (DD859/G of No 423 Sqn). Flg Off Albert Bishop put the aircraft down, but it dug in a float, cartwheeled on landing and began to burn. Five crewmen were killed in the crash, but the rest survived in their Mae Wests, and were able to watch the end of U-489, which approached them stern down, with most of the crew on the forward casing trying to balance it. But the U-Boat sank and its crew took to their dinghies, from which they regarded the Sunderland crew in silence until the arrival of HMS *Castleton*, which rescued both parties. Bishop won a DFC for the action.

As well as having to abandon 'fight back' tactics, the Germans were also forced to discontinue the use of their Metox radar warning receiver, having become convinced (quite erroneously) that aircraft were able to home on its radiation. The Naxos receiver (which detected Centimetric radar) was less effective, and the suspension left U-Boats more vulnerable still. A dispirited Dönitz recalled his boats altogether, and ceased group sailings.

With the dearth of U-Boats, the Sunderland crews entered a period of unproductive losses, since Luftwaffe opposition to their patrols was actually stepped up. And the destruction of U-Boats was now regarded as their most important role. On 7 September 1943, No 19 Group issued an instruction which confirmed this. 'The whole aim of the No 19 Group effort at the present time is the destruction of U-Boats . . . all other aims are to be subordinated to this aim'. The instruction also detailed the tactics and techniques to be used, but ignored the problems of what to do about fighter opposition.

On 8 August Flt Lt Norman Garrard of No 10 Sqn RAAF was attacked by six Ju 88s and escaped, but was shot down three days later. Flg Off

Although this photograph (taken on 27 August 1944) makes the surface of the Atlantic look like a mill-pond, a heavy swell was actually running at the time which threatened to pound Sunderland III EK573 to pieces when it took off. Flown by 'Port Melbournite' Flt Lt Bill Tilley of No 10 Sqn RAAF, the aircraft had alighted in order to rescue the survivors of a shot-down Wellington – their dinghy can be seen to the far right of the photo. A DFC winner, Tilley had previously sunk U-243 while flying W4030. This photo has been censored to remove all trace of the Sunderland's ASV gear. As with many war-weary Mk IIIs, EK573 finished its service career with No 4 (Coastal) OTU, before finally being struck off charge on 23 March 1947 *(via Phil Jarrett)*

Dowling of No 461 Sqn was lost on 13 August, Flt Lit Hickson Skinner of No 10 Sqn RAAF was shot down five days later, and on 30 August Flg Off C R Croft of No 461 Sqn fell to three Ju 88s, having survived an attack by three Junkers heavy fighters earlier during the same patrol.

A further flurry of losses to fighters began on 16 September when Dudley Mallows (on what was to have been his last 'op') was forced to ditch following a combat with six Ju 88s. He and his crew were rescued by the 2nd Destroyer Group (which had participated in Mallow's earlier sinking of U-461), and its commander was able to present the pilot with the lifejacket and survival gear of Kapitanleutnant Stiebler – the captain of that U-Boat! Five days later Flg Off Jennison of No 10 Sqn RAAF was downed by six Ju 88s, and on 2 October Flg Off Lees went missing after reporting engine trouble, unsuccessfully attempting to alight south of the Scillies.

Those Sunderlands that limped back to base with battle damage put an increasing strain on maintenance facilities, which were inevitably fairly primitive, and which were already somewhat over-stretched by the poor standard of new engines received from the supply chain. Indeed, one well-worn Sunderland on No 10 Sqn RAAF had to have seven different engines installed before it could be declared fit for operations.

Dönitz had kept most of his U-Boats out of the Atlantic since May, but he could not afford to let the vital convoys get through unmolested indefinitely. So, in August, he let loose a pack of 28 attack submarines and one *Milchkuh* tanker from bases in Norway and the Biscay ports. All had extra armour and defensive armament, new search radar receivers and two Zaunkoenig homing torpedoes for use against convoy escorts.

Despite warnings from decrypted *Ultra* traffic, the Allies were only able to sink one U-Boat before the submarines reached their patrol area, strung out in a long line across the convoy routes, waiting for westbound convoys ONS-18 and ONS-202. But the U-Boats were unlucky, losing 12 of their number to aircraft, although they were responsible for sinking seven freighters and four escorts. Operating at the limit of its range, Castle Archdale-based Sunderland DD863/J of No 423 Sqn, flown by Flg Off A H Russell, sank the Type VIIC U-610 on 8 October 1943.

While on convoy escort duties on 17 October, flying JM712/S, Flt Lt Paul Sargent of No 422 Sqn found U-470 and attacked. Two gunners

No 422 Sqn revelled in the nickname the 'Flying Yachtsmen', and one of its 'yachts' (ML884) was photographed at Pembroke Dock being taxied to a buoy by Flt Lt F B Fallis on 8 December 1944. A one-unit only aircraft, it shows obvious signs of having been recently re-coded. ML884 was actually the last in a batch of 50 Mk IIIs built by Blackburn Aircraft at Dumbarton between October 1943 and May 1944. No 422 Sqn ceased operating Sunderlands in June 1945, leaving ML884 to spend almost two years in storage before being struck off charge on 26 March 1947 *(via Andy Thomas)*

were killed during the second pass and the aircraft was badly damaged, but the U-Boat was lifted bodily out of the water before disappearing, and was presumed destroyed. Sargent then attempted to land his crippled Sunderland alongside the convoy, but the aircraft bounced and broke apart, and only seven men survived.

After a failed attempt by a Wolf Pack to interdict two Gibraltar-bound convoys in September, Dönitz ordered most of his U-Boats back to port for refit. This allowed him to introduce a new, potentially war-winning, device virtually fleet-wide. Known as the *Schnorkel*, it allowed U-Boats to stay submerged, running the diesel engines and re-charging the batteries at periscope depth, with only the periscope and 'snort' out of the water.

Fortunately, by late 1943 better (Centimetric) ASV radar was becoming available, and the new ASV Mk VIc was adopted for the Sunderland. This used split scanners in underwing radomes instead of Yagi aerials, dipoles and transmitter loops, reducing drag while also improving performance. With the new radar fitted, the aircraft became the Mk IIIA. But even with ASV Mk VIc, a submarine snorkel was a difficult radar target, and for the time being the initiative seemed to be with the U-Boats.

November and December 1943 were quiet months, however, although five aircraft were lost (one in a landing accident) during November and two during December. The November total very nearly reached six, however, with only good flying and excellent work from the gunners saving Flt Lt E Clark and DD865/L of No 10 Sqn RAAF from joining the statistics. Bounced by six Ju 88s, the aircraft was badly damaged in a 20-minute flight, although two of the attackers were driven off trailing smoke and flames. Clark gained the cover of cloud and flew home with no control of three engines (the throttle cables had been severed), which used up fuel at a prodigious rate. The engines cut out near the Lizard, and Clark made a successful deadstick landing on the sea, although the aircraft began shipping water. Fortunately, a passing trawler towed it back to Mount Batten before it could sink, giving No 10 Sqn's exhausted engineers more repair work to add to their already daunting workload!

Away from the frontline, the Sunderland Mk IV had been put in hand in 1942 to meet a perceived requirement for a faster, more powerful and more reliable version of the Sunderland to address remaining known

The Sunderland Mk IIIA combined the underwing radar scanners of the Mk V with the basic Mk III airframe. This aircraft (ML819) was photographed just prior to being delivered to the RAF from the Short Brothers & Harland factory at Belfast in mid-1944. A close examination of the photograph reveals the neater, lower drag radar installations outboard of either wing float. Issued to Norwegian-manned No 330 Sqn at Sullom Voe, ML819 was subsequently converted to full GR V specification and passed on to the *Aéronavale* on 30 August 1951 *(Author's collection)*

ML765 was Short's own Sunderland V prototype, which was augmented by the frontline conversion of ML839, as described in this chapter. Photographed at the company's Rochester works in March 1944, ML765 was eventually passed on to the MAEE, with whom it remained until struck off charge on 6 November 1947. As was typical for Ministry of Aircraft Production (MAP) photos taken during wartime, this shot has had its background completely removed by the MAP censor – indeed, the reverse side of this 1944-vintage print is stamped secret! *(via Phil Jarrett)*

shortcomings of the existing in-service variants. The large number of 0.303 in machine guns may have provided psychological comfort, but little real protection against fighters armed with heavy calibre machine guns or cannon, while the inadequate power of the Pegasus engines meant that these had to be operated at full boost for extended periods, with a commensurate effect on reliability. The lack of fully-feathering propellers also meant that they tended to tear away in flight after an engine failure, often causing severe damage. Two prototypes (MZ269 and MZ271) were built to meet Specification R.8/42, and a production batch of 40 aircraft (NJ200 to NJ239) were ordered at the same time.

The Mk IV was a minimum change derivative of the Mk III, with the same basic airframe and wing, but with four 1700 hp Bristol Hercules XIX engines driving new four-bladed fully-feathering airscrews, a 20 per cent larger tailplane (with 5° dihedral), a 39-in fuselage stretch, a redesigned planing bottom and improved armament. This consisted of a new FN 83 nose turret with twin 0.50 in Brownings, a Bristol B 17 mid-upper turret with twin 20 mm Hispano cannon and a Martin tail turret with two more 0.50 in Brownings. A further pair of 0.50 calibre machine guns were provided for the beam hatches, and a pair of fixed, forward-firing 0.303 in guns were mounted just above the chines on the nose. These latter fixed nose guns were the result of pressure from the frontline, and were intended to help suppress return fire from surfaced submarines. No 10 Sqn RAAF made a trial installation (on DD852/RB-J) in August 1943. Later, as a result of flight trials, the Mk IV prototype was fitted with an increased height, increased area tailfin with a dorsal fillet.

The first Sunderland IV prototype made its maiden flight on 30 August 1944 from Rochester, but it was already becoming clear that the war was drawing to a close, and the Mk IV offered too little improvement over the Mk V (already flying by then) to justify full production, and manufacture of the aircraft already on order was halted after only eight (plus the prototypes) had been completed. The type was re-named as the Seaford (perhaps in the hope that a new type would stand a better chance of being ordered than what might be perceived as a new incarnation of the 'ancient' Sunderland), but this had no real effect. The aircraft underwent operational trials with No 201 Sqn, were evaluated by Transport Command, and were finally converted as Solents for use by BOAC.

In the event, the replacement for the Sunderland III in Coastal Command service was the Mk V. Unusually, this new variant emerged (at least partly) from a service modification. The key problem with the Mk III was that its engines were insufficiently powerful, and because of this they were worked too hard, with a disastrous effect on reliability. Even when operated at full boost, the engines did not produce enough power to give the Sunderland anything more than modest performance characteristics, yet to fit larger, heavier, more powerful engines would be a major undertaking, and there were fears that the existing wing spars might not be sufficiently strong to permit such a modification.

Eventually, the station commander at Mount Batten, Gp Capt Jim Alexander (a former CO of No 10 Sqn RAAF), pressed for permission to modify a single aircraft with Pratt & Whitney R-1830-90 Twin Wasp engines driving fully-feathering airscrews. He discovered that Shorts were already working on the design of alternative engine installations, and had calculated that the Twin Wasp would not over-stress the existing wing spar. To his surprise, permission was granted, and while No 10 Sqn RAAF fitted one Sunderland (ML839/RB-A) with Twin Wasps, Shorts simultaneously produced their own conversion (ML765). The engines for the No 10 Sqn aircraft were supplied by the Ministry of Aircraft Production (MAP), but instruments and fittings were 'scrounged' from crashed Liberators elsewhere in Coastal Command, notably at St Eval.

ML839 sucessfully made its first flight with its new powerplants on 4 May 1944, although the RAAF pilots were not satisfied with the cropped propellers supplied by MAP, and scrounged new airscrews from a pair of Catalinas. The unit conducted 100 hours of test flying before ML839 began flying on ops – it was lost on 12 October, sinking at its moorings during a gale. Results of the experiment were passed on to Shorts, whose own conversion had flown for the first time in March 1944, and which had gone to the MAEE on 22 April.

The Mk V was rushed into production, and was identical to the late Mk IIIA, except in its powerplant installation. The new variant went to Nos 228 and 461 Sqns first, while No 10 Sqn RAAF, which had done so much to pioneer the modification, had to wait until after the war in Europe was over, receiving its first official GR Vs in June 1945.

The only real difference between the Sunderland IIIA and the Sunderland V lay in the engine installation, which made identifying one variant from the other extremely difficult. This aircraft has 'stickleback' exhaust shrouds fitted above the engine nacelles, which means that it is a Mk IIIA – the Mk V's exhaust stubs boasted no such attachment *(via Phil Jarrett)*

This Sunderland Mk V (PP105) was relatively unusual in retaining the Botha-type mid-upper gun turret, which became a rare sight during the closing months of the war. Built by Short Brothers at Rochester in late 1944, PP105 served initially with No 302 FTU before being passed on to No 209 Sqn, based at Kipevu, on the Kenyan coast. It was struck off charge on 10 March 1947
(via Phil Jarrett)

The Sunderland V marked a huge improvement over the original Pegasus-powered versions, with a top speed of 213 mph, an 18,000 ft ceiling and a radius of 430 miles. It was also able to fly home on any two engines, if necessary. But while this seemed like a major improvement, the expensive four-engined Sunderland still fell short of the performance achieved by the smaller and cheaper Catalina. To put the Sunderland V in context, it is only necessary to point out that while the Catalina was rather slower, it could climb to well above 20,000 ft and enjoyed a 600-mile radius.

If 1943 had seen the tide of the war in the Atlantic finally turn, then 1944 would see a consolidation of Allied successes (despite a few setbacks). Shorts would build 196 Sunderland during 1944, and with losses of aircraft and ships reducing, and U-Boat kills increasing, this success began to become more apparent.

The new year began with Dönitz deploying an arc of 22 U-Boats to cut the convoy routes to the UK. Unfortunately for the Germans, the Admiralty became aware of the plan and began hunting the enemy submarines down. Many were sunk by RN escorts, and then, on 8 January 1944, Flg Off J P Roberts of No 10 Sqn RAAF (flying EK586/U) sank the Type VIIC U-Boat U-426, for which he received a DFC.

Not to be outdone, No 461 Sqn sank another Type VIIC (U-571) later that month, on 28 January. The successful pilot was Flt Lt R D Lucas, commanding EK577/D, which was unusual in having a leaping kangaroo nose-art above the door, together with the legend *'HOP-ALONG'*. Three Sunderlands were lost during the month, probably all to enemy fighters.

February 1944 opened with Coastal Command having gained a new AOC-in-C in Air Chief Marshal Sir Sholto Douglas, who replaced Slessor on 20 January after the latter was posted to become Deputy Allied Air Commander in the Mediterranean. On the German side, Dönitz had replaced Raeder as C-in-C of the navy in January 1943, but still remained in overall charge of the U-Boat war, in which he continued to take a close personal interest.

Enemy fighters remained a real thorn in the side for the Sunderlands, with Flt Lt John McCulloch of No 10 Sqn RAAF gaining a record of sorts when his aircraft came under attack from 16 Ju 88s on 15 February. These split into gaggles of four and attacked from all points, but inflicted relatively light damage, although they did kill one of the Sunderland's gunners. The next day, an unidentified U-Boat was optimistically claimed as damaged by No 201 Sqn (EK594/W being the aircraft involved).

March was quiet, although on the 10th a new No 422 Sqn captain, WO W F Morton (flying EK591/U, and being screened by the experienced Flt Lt S R W Butler), attacked and sank U-625 despite intense flak, energetic zig-zagging and a low attack run. Before the crew abandoned their sinking Type VIIC, a message was flashed from the conning tower to the Sunderland. This was read off as 'F-I-N-E-B-O-M-B-I-S-H'.

Two days later a No 423 Sqn aircraft ditched, its crew being rescued, and on 20 March a No 330 Sqn Sunderland failed to return – probably falling to enemy fighters. But such incidents were uncommon, and even in May, in the run-up to D-Day, No 10 Sqn RAAF flew 52 sorties without sighting a single submarine, and only catching a glimpse of three enemy aircraft, none of which offered combat.

The introduction of the *Schnorkel* did not prevent the loss of 60 U-Boats for the destruction of only 54 allied ships in the first three months of 1944. Recognising the vulnerability of his Wolf Packs, Dönitz reluctantly ordered a change in tactics on 22 March, telling his U-Boat captains to operate autonomously and singly – making them more difficult to find, but also making them much less effective ship-killers.

From March 1944, the focus of Coastal Command's efforts again began to shift away from the Atlantic, with intelligence reports and *Ultra* confirming that the Germans were keeping back large numbers of submarines in anticipation of an Allied invasion of France. Sholto Douglas responded by maintaining day and night patrols over the western Channel and south-western approaches, since the eastern end of the Channel was more shallow and more heavily mined, and was only just over 20 miles wide at the Straits of Dover. These tactics paid off, and on the rare occasions that U-Boats penetrated into the Channel they were destroyed or driven off by the heavy concentration of ASW assets. These included six of the seven UK-based Sunderland units, with only No 330 Sqn remaining outside the operational area at Sullom Voe. Operation *Cork* effectively sealed off the Channel, with patrol aircraft crossing 12 designated zones at least once during every half hour.

Only one Sunderland crew made a U-Boat kill claim during April 1944. Captained by Flt Lt F G Fellows, the crew of DD862/A were credited with sinking U-311, although their actual victim was U-672, which was only damaged. On 6 May, Flt Lt Dick Cargeeg of No 10 Sqn RAAF was on patrol in DD853/J when its port outer propeller sheared off, damaging the port inner, which had to be shut down when it started running rough. At 1000 ft, 500 miles from base, things looked difficult, and the crew began jettisoning everything that was not fixed, including guns, ammunition and even floorboards. Cargeeg reached home and landed smoothly, albeit without enough fuel to taxy in to the moorings.

The first successful U-Boat attack of the month was undertaken on 16 May 1944 when 2Lt C T Johnsen of No 330 Sqn, flying JM667/V, attacked the surfaced U-240. The Type VIIC fought back hard, and members of both crews were killed and wounded in the exchange of fire. The submarine sank stern first, and the damaged aircraft returned to base with both starboard engines damaged, and two crew dead.

On 21 May 1944 Plt Off E T King of No 4 OTU attacked and damaged the Type VIIC submarine U-995, which had to return to port for repairs. The next confirmed U-Boat kill by a Sunderland was that of the U-675, a Type VIIC sunk on 24 May by ML736/R of No 4 OTU, commanded by Flt Lt T F P Frizzell DFC. Frizzell attacked down sun at 20 ft, releasing a stick of six depth charges, one of which hit the submarine's deck. The vessel's bows rose almost vertically out of the sea, and it then sank. The same day, Flt Lt R H Nesbitt of No 423 Sqn, flying DW111/S, attacked Type VIIC U-Boat U-921. Several of its crew were wounded and the damaged vessel was forced to return to base. Unfortunately, 24 May also saw the loss of a No 422 Sqn Sunderland, which failed to return from a patrol.

As the Allied invasion began, the German Naval Forces West Headquarters issued an order at 0500 on 6 June, bringing all U-Boats to immediate readiness and emphasising the vital importance of interdicting the invasion fleet, with the sentence 'Every boat that inflicts losses on the enemy while he is landing has fulfilled its primary purpose, even if it perishes in doing so'. Fifteen U-Boats (seven with *Schnorkels*) left Brest, although only three managed to penetrate into the Channel.

That night, two U-Boats were sunk by Sunderlands. Flt Lt C G D Lancaster of No 228 Sqn, flying ML877/R, attacked the Type VIIC U-970 by the glare of air-dropped flares, while Type VIIC U-955 was sunk by Flt Lt Les Baveystock in No 201 Sqn's ML760/S. The next Sunderland attack occurred on 11 June, when Flt Lt M E Slaughter of No 228 Sqn (flying ML880/U) depth charged U-333. The Sunderland was not heard from again, and was almost certainly downed by AA fire. U-333 survived for just over a month before being sunk by the Royal Navy.

July saw the first deployment of 'High Tea', a sonobuoy which could detect submarines underwater, although the equipment remained extremely rare and very secret. Coastal Command destroyed six U-Boats as they fled from their French bases in the face of the advance by the Allied armies, but 31 escaped. Eventually, with no Luftwaffe fighter bases in France, the danger posed by enemy aircraft virtually disappeared, and many Sunderlands operating over the Bay of Biscay had their mid-upper gun turrets removed.

In addition to the activity in and around the Channel, the U-Boat arm made a determined effort to break out into the Atlantic in June, with many submarines sailing from Norwegian and German bases. But the U-Boats were becoming vulner-

No 330 Sqn's Mk V ML827 is seen riding at anchor in Sullom Voe in April 1945. Delivered new to No 461 Sqn as a Mk III in mid-1944 (note the overpainting of the unit's '2' code number forward of the roundel), this aircraft was updated prior to being passed on to the Norwegian-manned squadron. ML827 was lost on 12 May 1945 when it ditched 100 miles south-west of the Faroe Islands after suffering engine failure (*via Andy Thomas*)

Pristine-looking Mk V RN282 shows off the last wartime camouflage scheme used by the Sunderland force. Note how the white undersides extend up and back over the leading edges. The aircraft wears the codes of No 461 Sqn, the Sunderland having been delivered new to the unit in early 1945. Enjoying a long postwar career, RN282 subsequently served with Nos 10 RAAF, 201, 88, 209 and 205 Sqns, before being struck off charge on 13 May 1958 (*via Andy Thomas*)

able in the open Atlantic (especially with the introduction of staggered box patrols, which crept forward at the speed of the convoys), and in October Dönitz began to concentrate his efforts closer in to Britain's coasts, off Cape Wrath, the Irish Sea and the Bristol and St George's Channels. By December, more than two-thirds of allied shipping losses (seven ships) were in UK coastal waters.

The next U-Boat to fall victim to a Sunderland was the Type VIIC U-243, sunk by Flt Lt Bill Tilley of No 10 Sqn RAAF on 8 July 1944. The submarine had been specifically ordered to stay on the surface and fight if attacked, and did so as W4030/H swept in at 75 ft to drop six depth charges. Several crew members continued firing as the submarine began to sink and men took to their liferafts. The doomed submarine was then attacked by a US Navy Liberator and a second No 10 Sqn RAAF Sunderland (JM684/K). Tilley dropped dinghies and food to the survivors, and guided the Canadian destroyer *Restigouche* to rescue them.

The next submarine to fall victim to a Sunderland was the Type IXC U-1222, lost with all hands on 11 July 1944. The vessel was submerged and using its *Schnorkel* when found by ML881/P of No 201 Sqn, captained by Flt Lt I F B Walters DFC. The U-Boat was depth-charged just as it prepared to dive, and was destroyed. Just over one week later, on 19 July, EJ155/O of No 330 Sqn attacked and damaged the U-387, a Type VIIC.

On 11 August Type VIIC U-385 released a radar decoy balloon, hoping to draw away any Allied aircraft. Unfortunately, the captain's timing was poor, and as Plt Off Ivan Southall of No 461 Sqn (in ML741/P) homed in on the balloon, he saw U-385 still on the surface, and hurriedly attacked it with six depth charges. Southall was unable to find the U-Boat, but he talked a surface group into the area, which finished it off.

On 12 August No 461 Sqn's Flg Off D A Little, in ML735/A, followed a similar pattern, finding, attacking and then losing sight of U-270, although when RN ships arrived at the scene, they found only survivors from the submarine, which had sunk. Six days later Type IXB U-107 became the second submarine destroyed by Les Baveystock of No 201 Sqn. After his first kill (in June), Baveystock had been granted compassionate leave and had rushed to London, where his father had just died. His crew were killed, with a stand-in captain, on their next op.

Soon after arriving in his patrol area, Baveystock was in the toilet of EJ150/W when his co-pilot sighted U-107's periscope – a veteran submarine responsible for sinking 39 ships. Regaining the second pilot's seat, Baveystock supervised the attack, which straddled the U-Boat with depth charges. This action won him a DSO to go with his DFC and DFM, making him one of the most highly decorated Sunderland pilots of the war.

On 26 August, Bill Tilley (who had destroyed U-243 on 8 July) found the survivors of a crashed Leigh Light Wellington, and landed to pick them up, taking off and returning to base successfully.

During the rest of 1944, Sunderlands encountered fewer and fewer U-Boats, although there were still isolated engagements. On 9 September Flg Off J N Farren of No 423 Sqn, flying ML825/D, saw vapour on the sea surface and picked up a faint wake, which he depth-charged. He homed three escort vessels to the position, but nothing was seen. U-484 was lost with all hands off the Inner Hebrides on this date, and was credited to the aircraft and ships of the Royal Canadian Navy, although some official sources do not credit the Sunderland.

One Sunderland that was officially credited with sharing in a U-Boat sinking was NJ188/G of No 330 Sqn, flown by Lt J Buer, who picked up a contact on radar on 25 November, but who was unable to bomb in the poor visibility. Instead, he called in a Liberator and a number of ships, which detected the submarine using Asdic, and then destroyed it. A U-Boat kill was officially credited to N9025/Y of No 201 Sqn, flown by Flt Lt D R Hatton, who depth charged a definite wake, and reported a large and spreading patch of oil. Two RN ships subsequently depth charged the oil slick, and a postwar reassessment (by the RN Historical Branch) credited the 6 December 1944 sinking of the U-297 to these ships. The last action of the year occurred on 28 December 1944, when No 423 Sqn claimed to have damaged an unidentified U-Boat.

Although their debut had been long delayed by Allied bombing, the Type XXI and Type XXIII U-Boats finally put to sea in 1945. And although 55 of the larger ocean-going Type XXIs and 35 coastal Type XXIIIs were in commission and working up by the end of 1944, the first Type XXI did not make an operational patrol until 30 April. The Type XXI was as fast underwater as most escort vessels, and was hard to detect and track, but its arrival was a classic example of too little too late. The Type XXIII was in service earlier, and the U-2322 claimed a British freighter on 25 February 1945. Although Dönitz kept dispatching U-Boats on anti-convoy patrols throughout early 1945, their losses became alarmingly high, and successes were few and far between.

Only one of the U-Boats claimed during 1945 was credited to a Sunderland, this being U-242, destroyed on 30 April by Flt Lt K H Foster in ML738/H of No 201 Sqn. Foster made several attacks on the submerged vessel, which was later finished off by RN ships.

Dönitz, as Hitler's successor, ordered the German armed forces to lay down their arms and surrender on 9 May 1945. The U-Boats were instructed to surface and, flying a black or blue surrender flag, to proceed to designated Allied ports. There was a real fear that some fanatical U-Boat commanders would not obey, and patrols continued until one minute after midnight on 4 June, when No 201 Sqn's CO, Wg Cdr J Barrett (of 1939 *Kensington Court* fame) received the order to return to base, marking the last operational patrol of the war.

Sunderland V RN304 was another aircraft that saw much frontline service postwar – it seen here wearing the 'NS' codes of No 201 Sqn in July 1949. This flying boat is, however, broadly representative of those aircraft which flew Coastal Command's last wartime missions. RN304 was struck off charge on 20 September 1957, having served out its final months in the RAF with the Flying Boat Training Squadron *(via Phil Jarrett)*

THE MEDITERRANEAN

Between the Wars, the RAF based many of its flying boat units in the Mediterranean, operating from a number of bases including Gibraltar, Malta, Alexandria No 228 Sqn. They performed Colonial Policing and 'showing the flag' missions, and protected Britain's vital trade routes to the Far East, via the Suez Canal and Arabian Gulf.

The RAF's third Sunderland unit to form was No 228 Sqn, which was always intended for service in the Mediterranean, and which moved out to Alexandria from 5 June 1939 after converting to the type at Pembroke Dock. But with the outbreak of war on 3 September, the Middle East looked more like a side-show, and five days later No 228 Sqn was ordered back to Pembroke Dock.

During the months of the 'Phoney War' the Mediterranean remained much as it had been between the wars, albeit with increased risk of U-Boat activity. This eventually prompted the despatch of No 230 Sqn at Seletar (which had been the first frontline unit to receive the type) to Alexandria, where it arrived on 6 May 1940. The fall of France and Italy's entry into the war changed the situation dramatically, giving the Axis easy access to the Mediterranean, and threatening Britain's supply line to India, the Far East and Australia. No 228 Sqn returned to the Mediterranean (to Malta) on 10 June (the day Italy entered the war), taking off for Alexandria at dawn the next day – just before its overnight moorings were bombed.

The Sunderlands began flying missions immediately, mainly searching for elements of the mighty Italian fleet, which outnumbered the Royal Navy within the Mediterranean. The first Sunderland pilot to engage the enemy with any effect was No 230 Sqn's 'Willie' Campbell, who had earlier written off an aircraft in Malaya. He attacked and sank the Italian submarine *Argonauta* at 1015 on 28 June 1940, dropping four 250-lb A/S bombs on the vessel. The CO of No 228 Sqn, Wg Cdr G E Nicholetts, DFC, was the next to make contact with an enemy submarine, attacking the *Anfitrite* just under four hours later. He damaged it sufficiently to force the vessel's return to base.

The next day, flying the same aircraft (L5804), Campbell scored again, this time attacking the *Rubino* and sinking it. While *Anfitrite* had been proceeding at periscope depth, the *Rubino* was on the surface, and was broken in half by the eight bombs dropped in two attacks. Campbell's submarine sinking the previous day had been

N6133 and N6135 of No 228 Sqn are seen at anchor at Kalafrana, Malta, wearing the unit's short-lived 'TO' series codes, and toned down national insignia. This photograph was taken just days after war had been declared, as the unit returned to Pembroke Dock on 10 September 1939. N6135 was written off upon landing at Pembroke Dock following the long ferry flight from Malta, its pilot being forced to alight downwind at the Welsh base due to poor weather. A float was lost during the recovery, and the Sunderland capsized and sank whilst attempts were being made to salvage the flying boat. N6133 lasted a little longer, going on to serve with No 201 Sqn until shot down by Bf 110s 90 miles south-west of Sumburgh, in the Shetland Islands, on 9 July 1940 *(via Bruce Robertson)*

met with some disbelief, and so after his second success he landed (in a swell with waves higher than the Sunderland's rear turret!) and picked up three survivors as 'proof'. He was awarded an immediate DFC. That same day Wg Cdr Nicholetts made another attack on an Italian submarine, straddling the *Sirena* with bombs but causing no damage. Twenty-four hours later, No 230 Sqn's Flt Lt Woodward (in L5803) attacked a destroyer off Tobruk, stopping it dead in the water. But this burst of activity and action was atypical, and submarine sightings remained rare.

The Sunderland units already had two enemies to deal with, for Vichy French air force units had also started operating against Britain from bases in the south of France and North Africa – especially after the Royal Navy's 3 July pre-emptive strike against French battleships at Oran. This uncomfortable operation had been mounted to remove the possibility of the French ships being used by, or on behalf of, the Germans – a sensible decision in the light of the widespread pro-German sentiment within the French navy, which went over to Vichy almost en-masse.

During a recce mission to Oran on 4 July Flt Lt Brooks' No 228 Sqn Sunderland (P9621) was attacked by three French Curtiss H-75As, although his crew downed one attacker and damaged another, which was claimed as a probable. One gunner was wounded, and the Sunderland was damaged, but it regained Gibraltar without further incident.

Both Mediterranean Sunderland units were involved in the first major battle between the Royal Navy and the Italian fleet on 9 July, aircraft shadowing the enemy fleet for much of the day as they guided RN warships towards their targets. The Battle of Punto Stilo was inconclusive, the Italians withdrawing from the engagement after one battleship was hit by HMS *Warspite*. During the day, Flt Lt Woodward of No 230 Sqn attacked and claimed a hit on an Italian submarine (probably *Zoea*), while Sqn Ldr Menzies of No 228 was fired on by AA and engaged in a 30-minute running fight with a Heinkel He 115, which eventually broke off.

Sqn Ldr Menzies attacked (and claimed to have sunk) an unidentified Italian submarine (probably *Settimo*) three days later. Postwar examination of Italian records revealed that the submarine had been lightly damaged by a Sunderland in the area on that day. The flying boats did not have things all their own way, with some missions attracting enemy fighter opposition – especially the regular recces of Augusta harbour on Sicily.

On 25 July a Sunderland flown by Flt Lt Garside was attacked by three CR.42s, and the crew shot one of the biplane fighters down and scored hits on another. However, the RAF aircraft was itself heavily damaged, and only just struggled back to Malta. On 28 July, another aircraft was bounced by three Macchi C.200s, and its crew claimed to have shot down one and forced another to break off with smoke pouring from its engine, before escaping without damage. Sqn Ldr Ryley of No 230 Sqn was less lucky, with three gunners being wounded during an hour-long engagement with four Macchis, one of which was again claimed as having been shot down.

By the time No 228 Sqn returned to the Mediterranean in June 1940, its aircraft wore standard camouflage and 'DQ' series codes, as shown here. This aircraft (L5806), seen alongside an ex-*Escadrille* 2HT Latécoere Laté 298B floatplane, was photographed at Kalafrana in July 1940. Aside from two spells with this unit, L5806 also served with Nos 210 and 230 Sqns prior to being lost on an anti-submarine patrol off the Egyptian coast on 25 July 1942. It was assigned to No 230 Sqn at the time *(via Andy Thomas)*

The Sunderland struggled back to Malta, where it was beached to avoid sinking – it was carrying *Daily Mail* correspondent, Alexander Clifford.

On 6 August the Mediterranean Sunderland units suffered their first loss when N9025/Y of No 228 Sqn, piloted by Flt Lt Thurston-Smith, fell to three CR.42s. The hydraulics were put out of action (crippling the turrets) and the port fuel tank set ablaze, but the aircraft force-landed successfully and was scuttled. The crew were taken prisoner by the Italian ships they had been shadowing. The aircraft had been sent out to relieve another Sunderland, and was to have 'homed in' a force of Swordfish torpedo bombers, although the mission had become a 'suicide job' once the ships came within easy range of their own land-based fighters.

The Sunderland turned aggressor on 17 September, when Sqn Ldr Menzies and his crew met a Cant Z.501 flying boat and shot it down in flames. On 30 September another Italian submarine, the *Gondar*, was

These No 228 Sqn Sunderlands are seen moored off the Greek coast during the evacuation of British forces in April 1941. Once full of fleeing Allied troops, they would head south for Crete. Note how the barrels from the four 0.303 in machine guns visible in this shot are already trained skyward in anticipation of a surprise attack by the Luftwaffe *(via Aeroplane)*

N9029 of No 228 Sqn flies over the Mediterranean during the Greek campaign. Serving solely with this unit, N9029 was later lost off the Egyptian coast during a patrol on 1 January 1943 *(via Phil Jarrett)*

sighted and engaged by the Australian naval vessel HMAS *Stuart*, which called in the Sunderland of Flt Lt Alington (L2166 of No 230 Sqn) when it ran out of depth charges. The pilot attacked, forcing the submarine to surface. It was then scuttled by its crew.

With two major convoys racing to reinforce Malta, the Royal Navy asked No 230 Sqn to monitor the Italian fleet in their Sicilian harbours, and provide warning if they should sail. The presence of an RN task force of 15 warships drew out four destroyers and three torpedo boats which, on 12 October, were located by the Sunderland of Sqn Ldr Woodward (which also had on board the No 230 Sqn OC, Wg Cdr Geoffrey Francis). The Sunderland led eight Swordfish in to attack the enemy fleet, and also guided RN warships towards their targets. The action resulted in the sinking of the destroyer *Artigliere*.

On 1 November No 228 Sqn lost N9020 (with Sqn Ldr Menzies and his crew) to a pair of Macchis, and nearly lost L5806 later that day when it was attacked by two Macchis and a CR.42. Flt Lit Ware earned a DFC by struggling back to Malta, while one of his gunners, LAC Barton, won a DFM for staying at his gun, despite his wounds, throughout the engagement. Italian forces invaded Greece in November 1940, but were beaten back, although they counter-attacked again in March 1941. From 7 March, anticipating such a move, the Allies began reinforcing Greece with convoys from North Africa. Hitler urged his ally to attack these convoys, and accordingly, on 26 March, the Battleship *Vittorio Veneto*, with eight cruisers and assorted destroyers, set sail. Aware of Italian intentions, the Royal Navy commander, Admiral Cunningham cleared the convoys and set sail with his own task group, consisting of the battleships *Barham*, *Valiant* and *Warspite*, the carrier *Formidable*, and nine destroyers.

Around dawn on 27 March, No 230 Sqn's Flt Lt McCall (in 'NM-P') reported sighting three cruisers, setting in motion what would become known as the Battle of Cape Matapan.

Another No 230 Sqn Sunderland involved in the battle was N9029 ('NM-V'), captained by Flt Lt Alan Lywood, which sighted the Italian force at around 0620. Lywood kept shuttling back and forth between the Italian and British fleets, sending reports to Admiral Cunningham and prompting the Italian commander, Admiral Iachino, to beg for fighters to 'get this shadowing aircraft off our backs as soon as possible'. No such help arrived, while an error by the Sunderland's navigator led directly to the discovery of a second fleet! The battle was swift and fierce, and resulted in damage to the *Vittorio Veneto*, which fled, and the sinking of the cruisers *Fiume*, *Pola* and *Zara*. Lywood was awarded a DFC for his part in the battle, which removed the major Italian naval threat in the Mediterranean for the rest of 1941.

The second assault on Greece brought with it participation by the Luftwaffe, and a virtual airborne siege of Malta. During March and early April four Sunderlands were strafed at their moorings at Kalafrana and St Paul's Bay, two of

A No 230 Sqn Sunderland I swings at anchor off Scaramanga, in Greece, during May 1941 (via Andy Thomas)

the aircraft being destroyed by rising star Oberleutnant Joachim Müncheberg in his Bf 109E. German participation in the invasion of Greece brought with it a rapid collapse, and the Sunderlands of Nos 228 and 230 Sqns were heavily involved in evacuating allied personnel, including the Greek royal family. Within weeks the Sunderlands were again evacuating British troops, this time from Crete back to Egypt in the face of the airborne invasion of the island. These operations demonstrated the rugged dependability of the Sunderland, and the type's sheer load-carrying capacity. On one occasion a single Sunderland carried 74 troops (and its ten-man crew) from Crete to Egypt.

Following the loss of Crete, No 228 Sqn was sent to Bathurst, West Africa (now the Gambia), leaving Egypt in dribs and drabs from 10 June. No 230 Sqn, however, remained in Egypt, although it moved from Alexandria to Aboukir. There was still a great deal of work to be done in the Mediterranean, protecting Malta and the convoys which aimed to resupply Allied forces in North Africa, while also countering axis convoys which were attempting to keep Rommel and the Italian armies resupplied. Enemy submarine activity intensified quite dramatically, and No 230 Sqn found itself working ever harder to try to oppose the threat.

On 1 August No 230 Sqn lost L2166 when it was downed by the Italian submarine *Delfino*, which was lightly damaged in the engagement, and which picked up the four surviving aircrewmen, including the captain, Flt Lt Brand. It was forced to abort its mission and return to base.

One of the unit's most successful Sunderland captains during late 1941 and early 1942 was Sqn Ldr Garside. On 21 October 1941 he made an unsuccessful series of attacks on *L'Atropo*, which escaped unharmed, but had more success on 9 January (in W3987/X) when he attacked and sank U-577. Garside made three more inconclusive attacks on submarines during January, and one in February, and was amongst the pilots who made a total of seven attacks during March and April. More attacks were made during May, including one by the newly-promoted Wg Cdr Garside, but again most of the submarines involved escaped relatively undamaged. The exception was the Italian *Argo*, which received hull and battery damage during Garside's attack on 27 May, forcing the captain to abandon his mission and remain on the surface. The next day the submarine was attacked again, first by Flt Lt G Pockley, flying W3983/R of No 10 Sqn RAAF, who caused further damage, and then by a number of Lockheed Hudsons. The submarine limped back to base.

The shattered remains of Sunderland I L2164 of No 228 Sqn lay in St Paul's Bay, Malta, on the evening of 10 March 1941, the aircraft having been set alight at its mooring by two Bf 109Es from 7./JG 26. It had been rendered immobile during a strafing attack by Messerschmitt fighters from the same *staffel* 72 hours earlier. One of its crew, Sgt A S Jones, was killed in the latter engagement whilst attempting to fight off the Bf 109Es with a solitary Vickers K gun. The aircraft sank when efforts were made to tow it ashore
(via Andy Thomas)

Operations continued to bring losses as well as successes, with T9050 of No 230 Sqn crashing on landing at Aboukir on 30 September, and T9071 of No 230 Sqn falling to a pair of Bf 110s near Benghazi on 21 December 1941. Its captain, Flt Lt S W R Hughes, pulled off a successful ditching near the coast and his crew and passengers waded ashore, where they were taken prisoner by Italian Carabineri – one of the passengers later succumbed to wounds inflicted during the fight. In the long march which followed, the roles were reversed, and Hughes found himself in command of 156 Italian prisoners, with whom he eventually regained allied lines!

Two more units operated briefly in the Mediterranean. No 204 Sqn spent about a month flying from Gibraltar while en route from Reykjavik to West Africa. The other outfit was No 202 Sqn, which had once been slated to be the third operational Sunderland unit, and had even received its first two aircraft, before conversion was cancelled. It finally began to receive Sunderlands (which operated alongside the unit's Catalinas) at Gibraltar from 20 December 1941, and these remained on strength until 20 September 1942, when the last sortie with the aircraft was flown. During its brief career as a 'partial' Sunderland operator, No 202 flew hundreds of sorties, and operated a total of 23 aircraft a few at a time.

During the period No 202 Sqn's Sunderlands attacked at least two Italian submarines, damaging the *Otaria* on 13 June 1942 (using a scratch No 10 Sqn RAAF 'ferry crew' under Sqn Ldr Reg Burrage in W4028/'AX-B') and then sinking the *Alabastro* on 14 September (using W6002/'AX-R', captained by Flt Lt E P Walshe). The unit may also have been responsible for the sinking of the *Veniero*, which disappeared sometime after 29 May, and which was attacked by the unit's 'M' (flown by Flg Off R M Corrie) on 7 June. His crew observed a large (300 x 150 yard) oil patch as well as foam and bubbles. No 202 Sqn was regularly reinforced by aircraft and crews from No 10 Sqn RAAF, but the Australian unit was never based at Gibraltar itself. A No 10 Sqn crew was responsible for an attack on the *Brin* on 6 June, but the submarine escaped undamaged.

The Sunderland presence in the Mediterranean ended in January 1943 with the move of No 230 Sqn to Dar-es-Salaam, in Tanganyika, although a six-aircraft detachment returned to Aboukir following Gen Alexander's victory in June 1943. The aircraft were used principally for transport duties, but also for ASR sweeps and SAR missions, with several night landings being made to pick up downed allied aircrew.

In a repeat of the 10 March incident, a *kette* of strafing Bf 109Es from 7./JG 26 (led by the *staffel's* ace of aces, Oberleutnant Joachim Müncheberg) destroyed No 228 Sqn's Sunderland I L5807 in Kalafrana harbour on 27 April 1941. The aircraft had just landed after guiding seven Hurricanes to Malta from the aircraft carrier HMS *Ark Royal* as part of Operation *Dunlop*. Plumes of acrid black smoke pour from the ruptured starboard wing tank of L2164 minutes after the strafing run (*via Bruce Robertson*)

Weakened by fire and cannon shell hits, the starboard wing buckled as the blaze grew in intensity. Soon totally consumed by fire, the aircraft swiftly sank. Amazingly, only one member of the Sunderland's crew was wounded in this attack (*via Andy Thomas*)

WEST AFRICA

By the end of 1940, the risk to British and allied shipping had increased. Pocket battleships and surface raiders had played havoc south of Gibraltar on a relatively limited scale during the early months of the war, with the U-Boats operating mainly in the Bay of Biscay and the Atlantic. By the end of 1940, however, the German submarines were ranging rather further afield, and had begun to chalk up successes off Africa's western shoreline. Protection for convoys as they transited along this long route became a priority, and on 15 January 1941, No 210 Sqn at Oban was ordered to detach three Sunderlands to Freetown, in Sierra Leone, where they would form No 95 Sqn. One aircraft force-landed in Portugal and was interned en route, but the detachment was ready to begin operations by 24 March 1941. The squadron subsequently formed a detachment at Bathurst in April 1941, which would eventually become the 'hub' of RAF operations in West Africa.

In June, No 228 Sqn at Aboukir, in Egypt, was ordered to move to Bathurst, but only two aircraft and a number of personnel made the move before the order was rescinded, and the remainder of the unit was sent back to the UK. Instead, No 204 Sqn moved down from Reykjavik to Bathurst, arriving on 28 August.

The greatest threat to the RAF Sunderlands in West Africa was posed by Vichy French aircraft in neighbouring French colonies. This was demonstrated on 29 September when two Sunderlands were attacked by French fighters, one suffering substantial damage and the death of its

Photographed at Pembroke Dock just prior to departing for West Africa in early 1941, Sunderland I L5802 is seen wearing the newly-applied codes of No 95 Sqn. The aircraft in the background (P9603) wears the 'RB' codes of No 10 Sqn RAAF. L5802 had seen service with Nos 210, 204 and 201 Sqns prior to being issued to No 95 Sqn, and it would go on to fly with No 461 Sqn before being relegated to No 4 (Coastal) OTU. It was lost in a night landing at Alness on 16 January 1943 whilst still serving with the training unit. By contrast, P9603 flew exclusively with No 10 Sqn RAAF, although it too was lost during a landing accident, this time at Pembroke Dock, on 24 June 1941 *(via Phil Jarrett)*

Sunderland I P9623/E of No 95 Sqn was interned in Portugal on 14 February 1941 after running out of fuel while en route to West Africa. The ex-No 210 Sqn machine was repaired, refloated and re-marked, entering Portuguese air force service as '136' *(via Andy Thomas)*

P9263 is seen in Lisbon harbour after being refloated. The original print of this photograph shows that the Sunderland was still wearing No 210 Sqn's 'DA' codes when it force-landed *(via Andy Thomas)*

Stripped of its camouflage, and wearing the Portuguese air force marking on its fuselage, '136' was photographed swinging at a mooring in 1945 *(via Andy Thomas)*

'third pilot', although the Sunderlands did shoot down one of their attackers. The Vichy French sometimes seemed to collaborate with the Germans and fight the British with rather more enthusiasm and courage than they had shown when trying to defend their country against the Germans, and fighters frequently attempted to shoot down patrolling RAF Sunderlands. No 95 Sqn accordingly organised a Hurricane fighter flight (which subsequently broke away to form No 128 Sqn).

The Sunderlands enjoyed little demonstrable success against enemy submarines, making few contacts and even fewer attacks, and failing to destroy a single enemy vessel. They did have an effect on the enemy,

No 95 Sqn commenced operations from Freetown on 24 March 1941, using this aircraft (N9050/D), captained by Flg Off S G Baggott. The unit's initial strength consisted of just three Sunderlands, although this was soon expanded to seven. This photo shows N9050 (formerly of No 10 Sqn RAAF) at No 95 Sqn's first moorings in West Africa, at Fourah Bay, in May 1941. A veteran of four frontline units (it served twice with No 95 Sqn), this Mk I ended its days with No 4 (Coastal) OTU, being struck off charge on 29 July 1944 *(via Andy Thomas)*

The very first production Sunderland, L2158 of No 204 Sqn is seen taking off from Bathurst in late 1941. The aircraft was lost on 17 August when it crashed during a convoy patrol off Sierra Leone on 17 August 1942. As its fuselage aerial 'farm' reveals, L2158 had been retrofitted with ASV radar (like all Sunderlands initially deployed to West Africa) *(via Bruce Robertson)*

however, and while Sunderland's were on patrol, not a single ship was lost within their range, and their arrival produced a dramatic reduction in shipping casualties. The greatest toll of Sunderlands was inflicted by engine failures, with at least seven aircraft being forced to land on the water, some doing so successfully, others being lost with all hands. Only two aircraft survived to be towed into port by friendly vessels.

Photographed in early 1942, No 204 Sqn's Sunderland I T9070 sits at moorings off the flying boat base at Bathurst, which was sited adjacent to Half Die Camp – so named because of the high death toll among the first white men to discover the place, which was swarming with malaria-infested mosquitoes. T9070 caught fire and blew up whilst moored off Half Die Camp on 16 August 1942 *(via Andy Thomas)*

No 95 Sqn's EJ144 is beached by Fisherman's Pier, near Port Etienne in the French protectorate of Mauretania, on 26 May 1943, having lost its port float during a forced landing. The pair of Sunderlands moored off in the distance brought in spares and maintenance 'troops' to effect the necessary repairs. Used exclusively by No 95 Sqn, this Mk III was later lost in a squall that struck the Bathurst moorings on 15 October 1944 *(via Bruce Robertson)*

Despite these engine problems, and despite the malaria and blackwater fever common around Bathurst, the Sunderland was destined to be used in significant numbers in West Africa. The next unit to arrive was No 343 (Free French) Sqn, which formed at Dakar in March 1943 as the 3rd and 4th *Escadrons* of *Flotille* 1, subsequently (in October) being re-designated as 7F. It was finally re-titled as No 343 Sqn in late November, when it came under RAF West Africa Command control.

One of the unit's pilots was an ex-Vichy French fighter pilot who had previously been awarded the Croix de Guerre for shooting down a Sunderland! A conversation with his instructor, Ray Gough, while converting at No 4 (Coastal) OTU, revealed that the Frenchman had

The end of the line for No 204 Sqn's Mk III JM680, which sank on landing at Half Die after hitting No 95 Sqn's Sunderland I W6062 on take-off on 31 May 1943. Perhaps surprisingly, in view of both its newness and apparent proximity to the shore, the aircraft was not recovered *(via Bruce Robertson)*

An excellent view of ASV-equipped Sunderland III ML837 in flight. This aircraft belonged to No 95 Sqn when photographed in 1944, and was struck off charge locally on 21 June 1945 *(via Andy Thomas)*

Sunderland III DV963 of No 95 Sqn takes off from Bathurst in 1944. Sunderlands based in West Africa wore the same camouflage and markings as those flying from the UK, although they soon appeared more 'sun-bleached'. During the early years of the campaign, the biggest danger to these aircraft was posed by Vichy French fighters, although the pilots of some of these aircraft later became Sunderland fliers themselves! DV963 served throughout its brief career with No 95 Sqn, being struck off charge on 13 July 1945 *(via Andy Thomas)*

been one of the Hawk pilots who attacked Gough's Sunderland (Gough had been the aircraft's co-pilot at the time) on 29 September 1941. Even more remarkably, the aircraft which he regularly flew on the course was N9044 – the very aircraft he'd claimed as a kill, still bearing the patched scars of its combat.

No 270 Sqn and No 490 Sqn RNZAF, both based at Jui, in Sierra Leone, replaced their Catalinas with Sunderlands from January and May 1944, respectively. These units continued their largely unsung work in West Africa until the end of the war, No s 95, 204 and 270 Sqns receiving disbandment orders in May 1945. After handing some aircraft to the French No 343 Sqn, the units destroyed their remaining aircraft by scuttling them on 21 June. No 490 Sqn continued until 1 August, when it disbanded at Jui. No 343 Sqn transferred back to the *Aéronavale* on 27 November 1945, becoming 7F once again.

No 95 Sqn Sunderland III JM671 was forced to ditch near Bathurst after suffering engine failure during a patrol in 1944. It was duly towed back to its moorings by the air force launch seen in the foreground. The RAF's 'sailors', who were formally organised as a Marine Branch after the war, were the unsung heroes of wartime Sunderland operations across the globe. This aircraft was eventually struck off charge on 21 June 1945, having flown only with No 95 Sqn *(via Phil Jarrett)*

OTHER THEATRES

itler's failure to knock Britain out of the war in 1940 meant that Germany was left fighting a global conflict, with Britain's maritime trade routes becoming an increasingly vital target for German U-Boats and surface raiders. Even before the Battle of France, the German navy began ranging far and wide as it hit out at British merchant ships. For example, the *Admiral Graf Spee* had moved into the Indian Ocean from the Atlantic in late 1939, returning to the Atlantic only because it had failed to find sufficient targets.

Even with the dominance of the British Fleet, finding such raiders in the great expanses of the world's ocean was a hit-and-miss affair, and increasing reliance was placed on maritime patrol aircraft for locating enemy warships, surface raiders, U-Boats and blockade-runners. But the main threat to British shipping in the early part of the war lay closer to home, and the Sunderland was a comparatively late entrant in the war against Japan, although it was not quite a newcomer to the Pacific region.

No 230 Sqn at Seletar had received Sunderlands in 1938 (becoming the first frontline unit to re-equip with the type), with its CO, Wg Cdr G M Bryer OBE, AFC flying out the first aircraft. With the importance of the flying boat to the Colonial Policing role, equipping units in the Far East and Mediterranean with Sunderlands was accorded a high priority. But once war broke out in Europe, the RAF's most modern maritime patrol aircraft were suddenly required for convoy escort and anti-submarine duties around Britain itself, and closer to home. With Italy's entry into the war, the Mediterranean also became a focus

In the early months of the Sunderland's war in the Pacific, the aircraft wore standard Coatsal Command markings and RAF roundels and fin flashes, as seen on No 230 Sqn's EJ143 at Kisumu, in Kenya, in 1943. This Mk III served exclusively with this unit, eventually being struck off charge on 12 March 1945 following two-and-a-half years of frontline flying *(via Andy Thomas)*

As aerial opposition was not a problem for Sunderlands operating in East Africa, they often flew without guns in order to boost the aircraft's modest performance. Seen in just such a configuration, this No 230 Sqn aircraft was photographed flying off Dar-es-Salaam in 1944 *(via Andy Thomas)*

of much attention, while the Far East declined in importance. Thus in May 1940 No 230 Sqn was moved to the Middle East, where the need for maritime patrol aircraft was now felt to be more pressing.

Japan's declaration of war did not result in an immediate deployment of Sunderlands to the Far East, and as a result the Royal Navy was handicapped in its efforts to stop the Japanese fleet by its lack of long range 'eyes'. Hong Kong, Malaya and Singapore fell to the Japanese, and then most of Burma, where the Japanese army was finally halted. Japan failed in its attempt to take or knock out Ceylon, and thereafter moved back from the Indian Ocean to the main body of the Pacific, but no-one could be sure as to whether pressure on the Indian Ocean would return, and British forces in the area were strengthened with this eventuality in mind.

1942 also saw the beginning of U-Boat operations (by the Eisbär Group) in the area, further increasing the need for patrol aircraft in the eastern Pacific and Indian Ocean. But the early reinforcements consisted of landplanes and Catalinas, and No 230 Sqn with Sunderlands did not return to the Pacific theatre until 9 January 1943.

The anti-submarine war in the Pacific was as fierce and barbaric as the rest of the conflict in that theatre, with many atrocities committed by Japanese submarine commanders, who routinely rammed or machine gunned survivors and lifeboats. Sometimes, they even took survivors onto their decks, where they were robbed of their possessions before being filmed being beaten, bludgeoned to death, stabbed, decapitated or shot, before being pushed overboard. Some were even less fortunate, being simply thrown overboard alive for the sharks.

Against these standards, the U-Boat commanders looked like a 'league of gentlemen', although they were no less difficult to find and sink. The Sunderland's part in the anti-submarine war in the Pacific was thus largely inconclusive, without a single confirmed submarine kill. But the lack of confirmed kills cannot tell the whole story, since the aircraft did close off large areas of ocean to enemy submarines, and severely restricted their operations, thereby saving countless tons of allied shipping.

No 209 Sqn would eventually receive Sunderlands, and although it was already 'in-theatre' based at Kipevu, in Kenya, in 1942, it was not the first Sunderland unit in the area. No 209 Sqn did not, in fact, become a Sunderland operator until 1944, and was not wholly Sunderland-equipped until February 1945.

No 230 Sqn's Mk III DP180 is seen in May 1944 at Dibougarh on a Casevac mission from its Koggala base. Nicknamed 'Gert', it was one of two squadron Sunderlands (the other was JM659/Q 'Daisy') detached from Koggala to the Brahmaputra River to ferry wounded Chindits back from Lake Myitkyina, near their base camp at Mosko. For 32 days the Sunderlands shuttled back and forth to Lake Myitkyina (which was miles inside enemy lines), lifting 537 men to safety. JM659 was written off at its moorings, while the aircraft pictured had a close escape when strafed by a Japanese fighter while taking off from Lake Myitkyina on its final mission. DP180 was finally struck off charge in January 1946 (via Andy Thomas)

All RAF aircraft operating in the Far East had the red in their national insignia removed to avoid the potential for confusion with Japan's 'meatball' insignia. No 230 Sqn's EJ143/S is seen at Koggala in late 1944 (via Bruce Robertson)

No 230 Sqn's Sunderland III JM673 (appropriately nicknamed 'Black Peter') was specially camouflaged for night anti-shipping missions in the Bay of Bengal – it is also illustrated in the colour profiles section. Delivered to No 230 Sqn fresh from Shorts' Rochester factory in early 1943, and flown primarily by the unit's OC, Wg Cdr D K Bednall, JM673 was posted missing on 28 November 1944 during a night patrol in bad weather
(via Andy Thomas)

No 259 Sqn enjoyed only the briefest existence as a Sunderland unit, re-equipping at Dar-es-Salaam in March 1945 before disbanding at the end of April! The aircraft in the distance undergoing engine maintenance belonged to this unit
(via Andy Thomas)

The first Sunderland unit in East Africa was thus No 230 Sqn, which had returned to the war in the East in January 1943, under the command of Wg Cdr Dundas Bednall. It had transferred to the beautiful palm-fringed harbour at Dar-es-Salaam, capital city of what was then Tanganyika. However picturesque the scenery, life in Dar-es-Salaam was hard, with dripping humidity and plagues of yellow fever and malaria-infested mosquitoes. Sickness was rife, and severely curtailed operations. Some detachments were even worse, with Tulear, in Madagascar, suffering an epidemic of gonorrhoea among its indigenous population, and where the disease inevitably spread to some of the RAF personnel – not least after it was discovered that a single tin of pilchards in tomato sauce was a more than acceptable price for a night of carnal pleasure! Cases of VD rose in direct proportion to the disappearance of canned pilchards from the insecure NAAFI stores.

The Sunderlands were often detached in threes or sixes to fly from distant bases, including Langebaan near Cape Town, Diego Garcia (a coral atoll in the Indian Ocean), Diego Suarez on Madagascar and Masirah Island off the coast of Oman. No 230 Sqn also sent detachments back to the Mediterranean, and from June 1943 maintained six aircraft at Aboukir.

Following a number of sinkings of British ships by U-Boats and Japanese submarines in the Indian Ocean, the focus of No 230 Sqn's attentions switched back to East Africa, and the unit flew a series of anti-submarine sweeps. By February 1944 the Allies had seized control of the Mediterranean and Indian Ocean, and the centre of gravity of the war against Japan moved further east. As the Burma campaign wore on, there was an increasing need for extra transport capacity in the region, and for ASV/ASW patrols in the Bay of Bengal and Andaman Sea. No 230 Sqn was consequently ordered to Koggala, Ceylon, flying there via Kisimu, Khartoum, Aden, Masirah, Korangi Creek, Bombay and Cochin. At Koggala No 230 Sqn joined a number of Catalina-equipped units, including No 205 Sqn, which would eventually convert to the Sunderland in June 1945.

No 230 Sqn's main task was now to conduct operations against Japanese coastal shipping involved in supporting enemy forces in Burma. But there were other tasks, too. In May 1944, for example, two aircraft were detached from Koggala to the Brahmaputra River,

from where they ferried wounded Chindits back from Lake Myitky-ina, near their base camp at Mosko. For 32 days the Sunderlands shuttled back and forth to Lake Myitky-ina (which was miles inside enemy lines), lifting 537 men to safety. One Sunderland was lost at its moorings and the other had a close escape when strafed by a Japanese fighter while taking off from Lake Myitkyina on its final mission.

The Sunderland itself was hard to keep serviceable in the tropics, and was not ideally suited to operations in Africa, the Indian Ocean and the Pacific. Engine reliability proved to be the biggest problem, which came as something of a surprise to the RAF. The Pegasus XVIII radial fitted to the Sunderland III had operated trouble-free in the Atlantic, and legend had it that BOAC had fewer problems with theirs on the East African routes by pumping suspect cylinders and valves with graphite grease. But on the RAF Sunderland IIIs in the Indian Ocean exhaust valves tended to stick, break off and then fall into the cylinder. The cylinder would then explode, or have a hole blown in it and the engine could stop. The propeller could not then be feathered, and would create massive drag, and would sometimes be torn off. The Sunderland was soon being described as a 'marvellous aircraft but those engines were just terrible! No good at all in the tropics'.

In fact, the engines were not at fault, nor did BOAC's fabled graphite grease have any more than a psychological effect. Postwar analysis showed that the problem was with local oil supplies (BOAC using supplies of oil

A rare shot of a No 259 Sqn Sunderland Mk V 'on the wing' off Mombasa in late March 1945. The unit's near-new flying boats were transferred to the South African Air Force when it disbanded at the end of the following month *(via Andy Thomas)*

As the war in the Pacific drew to a close, the need for South-East Asia Command (SEAC) type national insignia diminished. With the red and white colours restored to its national markings, No 209 Sqn's NJ261/T is seen over Mombasa on 28 April 1945. This aircraft survived the war only to be struck off charge on 30 May 1946 *(via Andy Thomas)*

shipped out from Britain), which allowed waxy deposits to build up on hot valve stems, causing them to stick and then be broken off by the rising pistons. The later Sunderland Mk Vs had Pratt & Whitney engines which were more tolerant of lower grade oil, and after an unrelated spate of early failures, suffered no problems in-theatre – although they were too late to make much difference to the course of the war.

No 230 Sqn began to receive Sunderland Vs in January 1945, and the unit's Mk IIIs were hastily ferried to Korangi Creek for storage. The new Mk Vs were delivered lacking a supercharger selector lever, so that the engines ran with superchargers (unnecessary in the tropics) operating all the time, causing failures after between 80 and 100 hours. The problem was discovered and the superchargers were disconnected and blanked off, and thereafter the Mk V was a great success.

Sunderland Vs delivered to the Far East (like these No 209 Sqn aircraft) did not use SEAC-type roundels, and also usually eschewed two-letter code prefixes *(via Andy Thomas)*

The new aircraft arrived just in time to participate in Mountbatten's liberation of Burma, which began with the capture of Rangoon in Operation *Dracula*. Four (later seven) Sunderlands were deployed to Akyab, and these transported freight to the 14th Army and flew anti-ship attacks in the Bay of Bengal, helping provide cover for the invasion fleet. In May 1945 the unit moved to Rangoon, from where it continued to fly anti-shipping attacks, ranging as far as the Malay Peninsula and the Gulf of Siam and claiming a number of enemy vessels sunk. Following the Japanese surrender, No 230 Sqn was heavily committed to the transport and trooping role.

Seen moored at Koggala in July 1945, this No 209 Sqn Mk V (NJ265) lacked a mid-upper gun turret, but did use the unit's 'WQ' code prefix. This aircraft later returned to the UK and served with No 235 (Flying Boat) OCU at Calshot, which in turn became the Flying Boat Training Squadron, at Pembroke Dock, in Ocotber 1953. NJ265 was finally struck off charge on 31 August 1955 *(via Andy Thomas)*

Although delivered with ASV radar, the six Sunderlands issued to the RAAF's No 40 Sqn at Townsville and Rathmines in early 1944 were used almost exclusively in the transport role, flying mainly between New Guinea and the Australian mainland. Four RNZAF Sunderland IIIs delivered to Hobsonville in late 1944 were similarly tasked, and played no active part in the fighting.

BOAC's C-Class 'Empire' Flying Boats saw occasional service in the war in the Pacific alongside their military cousins. On 19 July 1943, for example, *Cameronian* (G-AEUE), captained by Dick Reid, was en route from Dar-es-Salaam to Durban when it spotted a lifeboat from the torpedoed SS *City of Canton*. Against all regulations, Capt Reid landed (despite a modest swell) and picked up those survivors strong enough to be hauled by rope from their raft to the flying boat, then sent boats to pick up the remainder.

WARTIME CONCLUSION

The work of Coastal Command was never well publicised, and the extent of its contribution to Britain's war effort was never really recognised at the time. Fighter and Bomber Command seized the headlines and gained the recognition, and were also accorded a higher priority by politicians and air marshals alike. 'Bomber' Harris, for example, begrudged the diversion of any potential bombers to what he saw as a 'side-show', and was especially hostile to the Command receiving modern four-engined aircraft.

Ironically, credible (though controversial) postwar research has shown that a single four-engined bomber type aircraft operating with Coastal Command made 20 times the impact on the German war economy than a single Bomber Command Lancaster. It achieved this by inflicting direct damage on enemy ships and submarines, and through the economic dislocation caused by blockading Germany from vital raw materials. In the end, Coastal Command, and its allies, virtually prevented the German navy from conducting major surface operations. Most of its capital ships were sunk or holed-up in ports from which escape was impossible, and the U-Boat arm suffered horrifying losses. Many vital war materials were prevented from reaching Germany at all, forcing an increasing reliance on expensive and inferior synthetic alternatives.

The contribution of Coastal Command (and of maritime patrol aircraft operated by overseas Commands) was not limited to the way in which it was able to sink enemy ships and submarines, or the way in which it disrupted the import of strategic materials, however. Indeed, Coastal Command's primary purpose was defensive, maintaining reconnaissance patrols

The Sunderland V (in this case PP107), with its Twin Wasp engines, marked a great improvement over the Mk III, and proved notably superior in tropical climates. This No 209 Sqn aircraft is seen on its beaching trolley at Koggala in 1945. Later issued to No 205 Sqn, PP107 was lost on 28 January 1951 when it flew into Mount Morrison, near Hwalien on the island of Taiwan, after straying off course *(via Andy Thomas)*

No 205 Sqn was based at Koggala from 23 July 1942, and remained there for the rest of the war. Apart from a brief interlude at Iwakuni during 1950-51, the unit saw out the postwar Sunderland era at Seletar, Singapore, and was destined to be the RAF's last Sunderland squadron. Seen closest to the camera, Mk V SZ561 later served with the RNZAF *(via Andy Thomas)*

This No 205 Sqn aircraft (RN294/R) was photographed during a VJ-Day flypast over the Ceylonese captial of Colombo in September 1945. Returning to the UK postwar, the aircraft was later passed on to the Bombing Trials Unit at West Freugh. It was lost whilst still with this outfit on 20 December 1951 when it sank at its moorings at Wig Bay, near Stranraer *(via AS Thomas)*

which warned of hostile naval action (or, indeed, any invasion), and above all in protecting convoys. In protecting the convoys, Coastal Command aircraft kept the loss of friendly merchant ships to a sustainable level, thereby ensuring the maintenance of vital supplies to Britain. Some have expressed the belief that convoy protection and the sinking of enemy submarines was 'one and the same thing', but this was never the case. Sunderlands operating from African bases failed to score a single confirmed submarine kill, yet they fulfilled their task by preventing the enemy submarines from sinking hundreds of ships which might otherwise have been 'easy meat'.

And although the Sunderland may not have been the most effective aircraft type employed by Coastal Command during the war, its contribution was enormous, and there can be no doubt that the aircraft thoroughly deserved its place in history. And as if the Sunderland's magnificent wartime contribution were not enough, the type went on to give a further 14 years of invaluable frontline service to the RAF, participating in a number of combat operations, as detailed in the next chapter.

Photographs of the Sunderlands flown by No 40 Sqn RAAF are extremely rare, and have seldom been seen in print. The unit's aircraft wore an overall foliage green camouflage, with SEAC roundels and fin flash as seen here. This aircraft appears to have suffered serious damage both to its starboard wing trailing edge and port tailplane tip *(via Phil Jarrett)*

WAR AND PEACE

With the end of the war, Coastal Command found itself rapidly stripped of its most effective aircraft types, with the excellent Liberators and Catalinas being either returned to the USA or unceremoniously scrapped under the terms of lend-lease. The Halifax, meanwhile, had never enjoyed high-level support, and although the later Hercules engined Mk VI and Mk VII were superior to the Lancaster in many respects, the decision had been taken to withdraw the type from service, and only a handful lingered on in the Met reconnaissance role. This left the Sunderland as one of the mainstays of the peacetime Command's order of battle, and although Lancasters and Shackletons would soon come to dominate, the Sunderlands were destined to soldier on throughout the 1950s, albeit in limited numbers.

Between April and October 1945, ten RAF Sunderland units (Nos 10 RAAF, 95, 204, 228, 259, 270, 422, 423, 461 and 490 Sqns) were disbanded, and two more were transferred to their liberated nations (No 330 to Norway and No 343 to France), leaving six units (Nos 88, 201, 205, 209, 230 and 240 Sqns) operational. No 240 Sqn disappeared from the rolls in March 1946, leaving two UK-based Sunderland units and three overseas in Hong Kong, Ceylon and Singapore.

Existing stocks of Sunderlands were sufficient to support this depleted force, even after large-scale scrappings, and transfers of refurbished Sunderlands to foreign air forces. Production was therefore brought to a halt, the last aircraft from Rochester (TX293) flying on 27 September and Blackburn's final Sunderland (VB889) leaving the factory on 19 October. Finally, the last Belfast-built aircraft (SZ599) was launched on 14 June 1946. In fact, production of the civil Solent continued at Rochester until April 1948, although the factory closed for good soon afterwards.

There was certainly no need to continue with the Sunderland IV (by then re-named the Seaford), and only eight of the initial order (for 30 aircraft) were completed – most went either to No 201 Sqn or to

With the war over, many Sunderlands based overseas were scrapped locally, it being felt uneconomical to bring them all the way home to meet the same fate. Most were simply scuttled, without even being stripped of their engines or other useful spares. Here Mk III EK595/O, last used by the Iraq Communications Flight, meets a watery end off Khor Kuwait on 1 April 1946. A wartime veteran that had seen service with both Nos 201 and 422 Sqns following a short spell in Training Command, this aircraft had been damaged in a collision with a barge at Basra on 5 March and subsequently deemed uneconomical to repair (via Andy Thomas)

'TA' codes identify this smart GR 5 (SZ568) as belonging to No 235 (Coastal) OCU at Calshot. This unit was formed by the re-designation of No 4 (Coastal) OTU on 1 July 1947, and was retitled the Flying Boat Training Squadron on 17 October 1953 upon its move to Pembroke Dock. Delivered to the RAF in the late summer of 1945, SZ568 spent its entire life with training units before being struck off charge on 19 October 1956 *(via Phil Jarrett)*

Transport Command for brief trials, before being converted to civilian Solent 3 standards. The Seaford would have marked a significant improvement over any other military Sunderland version, with its longer fuselage and refined planing bottom, heavier, thicker gauge construction (permitting higher AUWs) and its Hercules 130 engines driving fully-feathering four-bladed propellers. Externally, the Seaford was distinguished by an increased height tail fin (with a dorsal fairing) and an increased area, dihedral tailplane. Internally, the new variant had double decks and accommodation for a seven-man crew and up to 30 passengers.

The first Sunderland 'exports' (apart from the transfers of Free French and Free Norwegian units home) were of 16 Mk Vs to the South African Air Force in March 1945 when the former No 262 Sqn at Congella, Durban, became No 35 Sqn SAAF, and re-equipped with Sunderlands. The South Africans operated the Sunderland until 8 October 1957.

As the Cold War began, the Sunderland soon found itself fulfilling vital new roles. During the Berlin Airlift, for example, Nos 201 and 230 Sqn shuttled between Finkenwerder (on the River Elbe) and Lake Havel in Berlin, bringing in $4^1/2$ tons of supplies on each trip, and flying out laden with manufactured goods and an eventual total of 1113 refugees (especially children). From July 1948 (when the operation began), Sunderlands ferried in 2500 tons of highly corrosive salt, which would have been difficult in aircraft not designed to operate in a salt-laden atmosphere.

RAF Sunderlands flew over 1000 sorties before Lake Havel froze over in December 1948, sometimes averaging 16 sorties per day. Turnaround times were rapid at 20 minutes (which might surprise anyone used to the aircraft's tiny doors and narrow gangways), and on one occasion a gang of 12 men unloaded 1020-lb of salt in only three minutes and twelve seconds! Military Sunderlands were augmented by three Hythes from the newly-formed Aquila Airways (whose founder was Barry Aikman, former CO of No 210 Sqn). The civil aircraft flew 265 sorties, lifting 1409 tons of supplies into the city. Airspace saturation prevented the Sunderland operation from re-starting when Havel thawed in the spring of 1949.

With three Sunderland units in the Far East (No 88 at Kai Tak, No 209 at Seletar, Singapore and No 205 at Koggala, Ceylon) the type was an early mainstay of Operation *Firedog*, launched on 17 June 1948. This

long-running (and eventually successful) operation was an anti-insurgency campaign intended to defeat the primarily Chinese Malayan Communist Party terrorists (or bandits) led by Chin Peng, who had been awarded the OBE for his part in resisting Japan's occupation of Malaysia. No 209 Sqn (joined at Seletar by No 205 in September 1949) flew in the bomber role, dropping small fragmentation bombs by hand through the aircraft hatches before proper bomb racks could be installed. The bomber role was eventually shouldered by detachments of Lancasters and Lincolns from UK-based Bomber Command units, and the Sunderlands returned to a coastal and maritime patrol role, searching, in particular for Chinese junks and freighters attempting to re-supply the terrorists.

The next emergency in which the Sunderland would become embroiled was the so-called Yangtse Incident. No 88 Sqn (initially formed at Kai Tak from No 1430 Flight on 1 September 1946) had already transitioned from its original transport role to that of general reconnaissance when the Korean War broke out in June 1950. For the first part of its existence, the unit had operated Sunderlands entirely stripped of armament and configured to carry 20 passengers,

Formed at Kai Tak from No 1430 Flight on 1 September 1946, No 88 Sqn was initially used only in the transport role. By the time GR 5 NJ176/F was photographed in 1949, however, No 88 Sqn was a fully-fledged maritime patrol unit, and would participate in the Korean War in the latter role. This aircraft was lost soon after this photo was taken when it swung of course during a night take-off in overloaded condition at Seletar on 21 November 1949 *(via Phil Jarrett)*

Wearing the codes 'B-P', No 230 Sqn's SZ567 flies over Greenland during the long operation mounted in support of the British North Greenland Expedition, conducted between 1951 and 1954 *(via Phil Jarrett)*

re-configuring its aircraft from April 1948 when BOAC took over the unit's routes. Even before the Korean War, one of the unit's aircraft (ML772/D) was involved in a famous and dramatic incident.

The Royal Navy frigate *Amethyst* was damaged and became trapped by Communist forces as it tried to navigate down the Yangtse river. Attempts by HMS *Blake* and HMS *London* to reach the vessel failed, and the RAF were called in. From 21 September 1949, the Sunderland, captained by Flt Lt Ken Letford DSO, DFC, took supplies and a doctor to the *Amethyst*, landing twice, but coming under heavy and accurate machine gun fire each time. Letford received a bar to his DFC for the operation, and *Amethyst* made a successful run for the open sea. In May 1949 No 88 Sqn flew several sorties to evacuate 121 British nationals from Shanghai – the mission *Amethyst* had been assigned to undertake.

All three FEAF Sunderland units were to be involved in the Korean War, rotating detachments through Iwakuni, Japan, for 15-hour day and night patrols off Korea's coasts. No 88 Sqn initially participated in both *Firedog* and the Korean operations, but thereafter became fully committed to the Korean War, including flying troops to Japan. The unit operated from Kai Tak and Iwakuni for about a year, before withdrawing to Seletar, Singapore, to join the other flying boat units.

In the UK, Sunderland operations continued well into the 1950s. No 4 (Coastal Command) OTU at Calshot was re-designated No 235 OCU in 1947, and retained Sunderlands until 1953, while No s201 and 230 Sqns served at Pembroke Dock until 1957, latterly with the Flying Boat Training Squadron, which took over from No 235 OCU. One of the

No 201 Sqn's DP198/A was moored in the Pool of London by Tower Bridge for the Battle of Britain Week celebrations in September 1956. The Squadron disbanded on 28 February 1957, followed on 31 July by the remaining UK-based Sunderland unit, No 230 Sqn. Built by Shorts at its Windermere factory as a Mk III in late 1943, DP198 had served with No 423 Sqn during the war. Converted to GR 5 configuration in 1945, it was subsequently operated by Nos 209, 205 and 201 Sqns, with the latter unit passing it back to No 205 Sqn in 1957 for further service in the Far East. DP198 was finally struck off charge on 30 June 1959 at Changi, by which time it was one of just two Sunderlands still in operational service with the RAF
(via Phil Jarrett)

The Sunderland graveyard at Seletar following the final retirement of the flying boat from No 205/209 Sqn in 1959. The aircrafts' Pratt & Whitney Twin Wasp engines still had some commercial value, so were removed, but the big flying boats themselves were quickly and ignominiously broken up for scrap. Plans to preserve one were foiled by the lack of flying boat bases between Singapore and the UK. The GR 5 to the right of this photograph (PP137) had been a resident of the graveyard since it was struck off charge on 11 February 1957 *(via Phil Jarrett)*

The French *Aéronavale* kept its Sunderlands in service into the 1960s, when they were finally retired. Three ended up being preserved, two of them in Britain. Ex-No 201 Sqn and No 235 (Coastal) OCU GR 5 RN284 was no one of them, however *(via Phil Jarrett)*

most high profile tasks carried out by the UK-based Sunderland units was support for the British North Greenland Expedition.

No 230 Sqn ferried in 150 tons of supplies from Young Sound in Eastern Greenland to base camp (Britannia Lake) in 1952, with No 201 taking over the resupply effort during 1953, before No 230 finally brought the expedition home in 1954. The Sunderlands 'left behind' at Pembroke Dock' were by no means idle, however, and flew innumerable search and rescue and relief operations, in addition to the normal round of ASW training. In August 1953, for example, a No 230 Sqn detachment in Malta flew medical supplies and personnel into the affected area following an earthquake in the Greek Ionian islands.

The two UK-based Sunderland units were disbanded on 28 February 1957 (No 201 Sqn) and 31 July 1957 (No 230 Sqn), their aircraft passing to Wig Bay for storage and possible issue to the FEAF Sunderland unit, before finally being disposed of for scrap. Despite public pressure, not one was allocated for preservation.

Back in the Far East, *Firedog* continued long after the Korean War ground to a halt on 27 July 1953, following the signing of the Panmunjom armistice agreement. No 88 Sqn disbanded on 1 October 1954, although the remaining units continued to operate in support of *Firedog*. But attrition reduced the number of available Sunderlands, and on 1 January 1955 the two FEAF units merged to form the single No 205/209 Sqn, this later becoming No 209 Sqn Detachment from 1 March 1958.

The FEAF unit's last aircraft made a final farewell flypast on 15 May 1959 (led by ML797), the day after DP198 (captained by Flt Lt Ben Ford) had flown the historic last 'op'. ML797 (the RAF's last flying Sunderland) completed a final non-operational sortie five days later. The RAF went as far as to earmark ML797/P for preservation, but these plans were cancelled due to the lack of flying boat bases on the route back to the UK, and the aircraft was struck off charge and scrapped on 30 June 1959.

But the disbandment of No 205 (205/209) Sqn did not mark the final retirement of the Sunderland, and nor did the scrapping of its aircraft mark the disappearance of the breed.

The Free French No 343 Sqn had been transferred to the *Aéronavale*, with its Sunderlands, in November 1945, forming *Flotille* 7FE at Dakar, in Senegal. Further batches of Sunderlands were acquired 'second-hand', allowing the re-equipment of 12S, 50S and 53S, while 7FE was redesignated first as 7F, then as 27F. Three Sunderlands (all ex-RAF) remained operational with the *Aéronavale* in Dakar until late 1960.

These aircraft were then flown back to France (Lanveoc-Poulmic, near Brest), where they served with 50S. One of the survivors was duly presented to the Sunderland trust for display at Pembroke Dock, flying back to Britain on 24 March 1961. This aircraft (ML824) subsequently found its way to the RAF Museum at Hendon in 1971, where it remains. Two flying boats remained in French service until 30 January 1962, with one aircraft (ML796) eventually becoming a (grounded, shore-based) discotheque and bar at La Baule, in Brittany, before being saved for preservation at the Imperial War Museum at Duxford in 1976. Even this *Aéronavale* interlude was not quite the end of the line for the big Short flying boat.

The RNZAF had acquired 16 refurbished Sunderland Mk Vs in 1952, equipping Nos 5 and 6 Sqns at Lauthala, in Fiji, and at Hobsonville. No 6 Sqn became the Maritime OCU and later the Maritime Reconnaissance and Support Unit (MRSU). In February 1965 No 5 Sqn moved back to Hobsonville with its four Sunderlands (reduced from six in April 1962), absorbing the disbanding MRSU and its three remaining aircraft. Sunderland conversion training ceased in October 1965, and the Fiji detachment of aircraft was reduced from two to one in 1966.

The RNZAF finally retired its last Sunderland (NZ4107, ex-VB883) on 2 April 1967, this marking the return of the remaining Fiji-based aircraft to Hobsonville on the closure of RNZAF Lauthala. One ex-RNZAF Sunderland was passed to Ansett at VH-BRF, and one more was retired to the Auckland Museum of Transport and Technology.

A handful of aircraft converted to Sandringham standards served with Antilles Air Boats in the Virgin Islands into the 1970s. One of these still remains airworthy as part of Kermit Weeks' incredible collection of historic aircraft in Florida, although it seldom flies.

TRANSPORTS AND AIRLINERS

On the outbreak of war, the Royal Air Force had no separate Transport Command, relying instead on a single communications squadron (No 24, at Northolt) and a number of bomber-transport units flying largely obsolete aircraft like the Bombay and Valentia. All civil flying in Britain officially ended on 3 September 1939 (the day that war was declared), although Imperial Airways and British Airways continued to operate certain vital routes under the direction of the Air Ministry. The two rival companies were amalgamated under a British Overseas Airways Corporation Act on 24 November 1939, and began operating as BOAC in April 1940.

Although the civil airlines continued, they did so much reduced in strength, with many personnel transferring to the 'fighting services' and most of their useful aircraft types being impressed for military transport duties. These included several of the former Imperial Airways 'Empire' (C-Class) flying boats from which the Sunderland was derived, and some of the improved 'Golden Hind' (G-Class) boats. The C-Class boats were produced in three sub-variants: the basic S 23 with 920 hp Pegasus XC engines; the strengthened, higher All Up Weight (AUW) S 26, with 890 hp Perseus XIIC engines in lower drag nacelles; and the S 33 with Pegasus XI engines and the original lower AUW limit.

Those civil Short flying boats passed to the military included S 23 G-AETY *Clio* (which became AX659), S 23 G-AEUD *Cordelia* (which became AX660), S 30 G-AFCU *Cabot* (which became V3137) and S 30 G-AFCV *Caribou* (which became V3138). S 33 G-AFPZ *Clifton*,

With its turrets removed and faired over, and wearing a prominent civil registration, Rochester-built BOAC Sunderland G-AGHZ *Hawkesbury* was the former Mk III ML727, which did not become G-AGHY as is often reported – the latter registration remained unallocated *(via Phil Jarrett)*

meanwhile, became A18-14 with the RAAF. All three G-Class flying boats (S 26s G-AFCI, FCJ and FCK – *Golden Hind, Golden Fleece* and *Golden Horn,* respectively) were impressed as X8275, X8274 and X8273. And despite the fact that these aircraft had been built as luxury airliners, some were fitted out for full ASW operations with gun turrets and ASV radar, while others fulfilled the military transport role.

The remaining C-Class boats taken over by BOAC (about 17 aircraft), and a smaller number used by Qantas Empire Airways and impressed by the Australian Government, went into service transporting essential personnel over routes to South and West Africa, Egypt and the Far East, albeit with rather more spartan interiors than had been fitted during Imperial Airways days. Throughout 1940 and into 1941, Coastal Command needed every Sunderland it could lay its hands on, and there were none spare for BOAC – even to replace the steady attrition of the hard-worked Empire boats, except on short-term loan.

But this changed in December 1942, when six Sunderland IIIs (JM660 to JM665) emerged from Rochester in standard BOAC camouflage, and wearing civil registrations G-AGER, S, T, U, V and W. These aircraft were stripped of gun turrets (with a retractable fairing replacing the front turret), and had an austere bench-seating fit installed. By September 1943, BOAC had received six more Sunderlands (G-AGHV/JM722 and G-AGHW, X, Y, and G-AGIA and B – ML725 to ML 729), and these were used principally on the route to West Africa.

From October 1943, the aircraft were used more on the route to Karachi, and used temporary military codes between OQZA and OQZZ for flights through militarised zones (Egypt). In mid 1944, BOAC received six more Sunderlands (ML786 to ML791), bringing the total to 16 (two had been lost in accidents). In BOAC wartime service, the Sunderlands enjoyed an excellent reputation, and despite being used on the peripheries of enemy airspace, none were lost as a result of enemy action.

After the war, the surviving BOAC Sunderlands were repainted (white overall) and re-fitted with airline standard seats as the Hythe-class, or were more extensively rebuilt (with streamlined noses and tails, more and larger windows and with seating for 24 passengers, provision for 6500-lb of air mail, ladies powder room, eight convertible sleeping berths and a cocktail bar) as the Sandringham-class.

BOAC retired the Hythes in February 1949, and the Sandringham and Seaford-based Solent bowed out when the airline ceased flying boat operations in November 1950. Aquila Airlines continued operating Hythes and Solents until 1958, when the career of the UK-based Sunderland finally drew to a close.

But BOAC's validation of the 'civilianised' Sunderland reinforced the type's credibility, and relatively large numbers were exported to Argentina (*Compania Argentina de Aeronavegacion Dodero,* later absorbed by *Aerolineas Argentineas*), Australia (Qantas, Trans Oceanic Airways, Barrier Reef Airways, Ansett), France (*France Hydro and Reseau Aerien Interinsulaire*), New Zealand (Tasman Empire Airlines Ltd and New Zealand National Airways Corporation), Norway (DNL), Portugal and Uruguay (*Compania Aeronautica Uruguayana SA – CAUSA*).

Aerolineas Argentinas eventually received 11 Sunderlands of various types (including three from *CAUSA*), and retired the six survivors in

1962, after which *Co-operative Argentina de Aeronavegantes* used them for freight services until January 1967.

In Australia, QANTAS itself briefly operated five Sunderlands at the start of the 1950s, but soon retired them. TOA flew three ex-RAAF Sunderlands converted to Hythe configuration from 1947, subsequently receiving three Solents. The company went into liquidation in April 1953, after which two of the TOA Solents were sold in the USA, although these remained unflown in desert storage throughout the 1960s and 1970s. One aircraft flew briefly with Ansett (until March 1954), this operator having been formed through a merger of Barrier Reef Airways and Ansett Airways – the latter acquired Barrier Reef's single ex-QANTAS aircraft and four ex-TEAL machines. Ansett continued operating the flying boats until 1974, when two were sold to Antilles Air Boats in the Virgin Islands. Another Australian-registered Sunderland was used for charter work around New Guinea until 1958, when it was registered to the French Polynesian *Reseau Aerien Interinsulaire*. This aircraft was finally retired (to the *Musée de l'Air* at Le Bourget) in 1970.

TEAL (Tasman Empire Airlines Ltd) originally flew four Twin-Wasp powered Sandringhams, which were soon replaced by five Solents – these operated until September 1960. New Zealand National Airways Corporation used four ex-RNZAF Sunderland IIIs until the mid-1950s.

The Norwegian airline DNL used three Sandringhams from 1946, acquiring two more as attrition replacements (the original three were all written off) before phasing the type out in 1951, when absorbed into SAS. The two survivors went to *Aerolineas Argentinas* and *France Hydro*.

The last Sunderlands of any sort to remain in productive revenue-earning service were the two aircraft operated by Antilles Air Boats in the Virgin Islands. Both returned to the UK in 1981, following the 1980 death of the airline's owner, Charles Blair, in the crash of a Grumman Goose. One was restored and placed in the Southampton Hall of Aviation, while the other returned to airworthy condition, and eventually found its way into the collection of wealthy US warbird operator, Kermit Weeks, in 1990.

Stripped of camouflage, the BOAC Sunderlands reverted to four-letter Transport Command codes in 1943 to allow them to fly through Egyptian airspace – this aircraft is OOZB. The author's father-in-law (then a humble sergeant in the Intelligence Corps) enjoyed the luxury of a journey back from India in one of these magnificent machines, and remembers the well-appointed cabin to this day! *(Author's Collection)*

APPENDICES

APPENDIX A

RAF SUNDERLAND UNITS

No 88 Sqn

No 88 Sqn was formed at Kai Tak on 1 September 1946 from No 1430 Flight. The unit moved to Seletar, Singapore, on 24 June 1951 after operating from Iwakuni during the Korean War. The unit disbanded on 1 October 1954, subsequently becoming a Canberra interdictor squadron in RAF Germany. Code RH-

No 95 Sqn

No 95 Sqn formed at Oban on 15 January 1941, and moved to Pembroke Dock on 16 January 1941. The unit transferred to Freetown, Sierra Leone, on 17 March 1941, and began operations on 24 March. It moved to Jui on 9 April 1942, and to Bathurst on 7 March 1943. The squadron ceased flying on 25 May 1945 and disbanded at Bathurst on 30 June 1945. Codes were SE- and DE-

No 119 Sqn

No 119 Sqn re-formed at Bowmore on 13 March 1941 from G Flight, which had, in turn, been formed to operate the G-Class flying boats taken over from Imperial Airways. The unit also briefly used two C-Class boats. Becoming non-operational, it re-formed at Lough Erne in April 1942 with Catalinas, then its crews were allocated to ferry Catalinas. The unit then reassembled, re-forming at Pembroke Dock and flying its first mission with Sunderlands on 20 November 1942. The squadron was disbanded on 17 April 1943. Code NH-

No 201 Sqn

No 201 Sqn converted to the Sunderland (from the Saro London) after receiving its first pair of aircraft at Invergordon on 13 April 1940. The squadron moved to Lough Erne on 18 September 1941, then to Pembroke Dock between 3 March and 3 November 1944. It returned to Pembroke Dock on 3 August 1945, moved to Calshot on 1 April 1946 and then back to Pembroke Dock on 17 January 1949. The unit finally disbanded on 28 February 1957.

No 201 Sqn's U-Boat claims included U-107, U-242, (U-297), U-440, U-518 (damaged), U-631, U-955 and U-1222. Submarine-killing aircraft used by No 201 Sqn were N9025/Y (U-297), W6005/P (U-518), W6051/T (U-631), DD835/R (U-440), EJ150/W (U-107), EK594/W (unidentified U-Boat), ML738/H (U-242), ML760/S (U-955) and ML881/P (U-1222).

Wartime codes were ZM- and NS-, and postwar A- and 201-

No 202 Sqn

No 202 Sqn began converting to the Sunderland in April 1939 at Kalafrana, Malta, but this was cancelled. It finally received Sunderlands at Gibraltar over two-and-half-years later, operating them from 20 December 1941 through to 20 September 1942, when the squadron re-equipped with Catalinas.

No 202 Sqn's submarine claims included the U-384, U-527, *Alabastro* and *Otaria* (damaged). Submarine-killing aircraft used by the unit were W4028/B (*Otaria*), W6002/R (*Alabastro*) and DD829/Z (U-384 and U-527).

Codes were TQ- and AX-

No 204 Sqn

No 204 Sqn at Mount Batten received its first Sunderland on 8 June 1939, converting from the Saro London. It moved to Sullom Voe on 2 April 1940, to Reykjavik on 5 April 1941, to Bathurst on 28 August and on to Jui on 28 January 1944, where it disbanded on 30 June 1945. Codes were RF- and KG-

No 205 Sqn

No 205 Sqn converted from Catalinas to Sunderlands at Koggala, Ceylon, in June 1945, moving to Seletar, on 15 September 1949, and remaining there (apart from a brief stay at Iwakuni between October and May 1951) until it absorbed No 209 Sqn in 1955. It was thereafter known as No 205/209 Sqn. The unit flew its last Sunderland sorties in May 1959, replacing the flying boats with Shackletons. Codes were FV- and KM-

No 209 Sqn

No 209 Sqn converted to the Sunderland in February 1945 at Kipevu, Kenya (having previously operated single Sunderlands alongside its Catalinas on a number of occasions). The unit moved to Koggala on 21 July 1945, to Kai Tak on 17 September and on to Seletar on 28 April 1946. No 209 Sqn merged with No 205 on 1 January 1955. Code WQ-

No 210 Sqn

Although No 230 Sqn would receive the RAF's first Sunderlands on 25 June 1938, they were flown out to Singapore by a No 210 Sqn crew! No 210 Sqn at Pembroke Dock received its first aircraft the next month (3 July 1938). Briefly based at Tayport in October 1938, the unit moved on to Invergordon and finally to Oban on 13 July 1940. It converted to Catalinas in April 1941.

No 210 Sqn's submarine claims included U-51 (damaged) and *Marcello*. Submarine-killing aircraft used by No 210 included P9624/H (U-51 and *Marcello*).

Codes were VG- and DA-

No 228 Sqn

No 228 Sqn replaced its Stranraers with Sunderlands in November 1938 at Pembroke Dock. The unit moved to Alexandria on 5 June 1939, but then returned to Pembroke Dock on 10 September following the declaration of war.

The unit returned to the Mediterranean (to Alexandria) in June 1940, moving to Aboukir in September. Based at Kalafrana from 13 September, No 228 returned to Aboukir in March, and then moved to Bathurst in West Africa in August 1941. The unit returned to Britain in October, moving to Oban in March 1942 and to Lough Erne in December 1942. A final move was made to Pembroke Dock in May 1943, where the unit disbanded on 4 June 1945, later reappearing as a Shackleton squadron.

No 228's submarine claims included U-55 (shared), U-106, U-333 (damaged), U-383, U-441 (damaged), U-563 (shared), U-564 (damaged), U-607, U-608, U-970 and *Anfitrite*. Submarine-killing aircraft used by No 228 were DD837/V (U-608), DD838/X (U-563), DV967/U (U-564), EJ139/L (U-441), JM678/V (U-383), JM708/N (U-106, U-607), ML877/R (U-970), ML880/U (U-333), and ML882/Y (U-55).

Codes were TO-, BH-, NM-, DQ- and 1-

No 230 Sqn

No 230 Sqn at Seletar began conversion to the Sunderland in June 1938, and made a number of moves first to Penang on 15 October 1939 and then to Koggala in February 1940. Although based at Alexandria from May 1940, the unit maintained detachments at Malta, Suda Bay (Crete) and Scaramanga, before moving to Aboukir in June 1941. No 230 then turned its attention to the Pacific and Indian Oceans, moving to Dar-es-Salaam in January 1943. It moved back to Koggala in February 1944, and then to Akyab in April 1945, to Redhills Lake in July 1945 and finally to Seletar on 30 November 1945. The unit returned to Castle Archdale in March 1946, before taking up station at Calshot the following month. No 230's last home was Pembroke Dock (from February 1949), where it disbanded as the last UK-based Sunderland unit on 31 July 1957.

No 230's submarine claims included U-577, *Argonauta*, *Gondar* (shared) and *Rubino*. Submarine-killing aircraft used by No 230 were L2166 (*Gondar*), L5804/S (*Argonauta* and *Rubino*) and W3987/X (U-577).

Codes were FV-, 4X- and B-

No 240 Sqn

No 240 Sqn at Redhills Lake began trading Catalinas for Sunderlands in July 1945, but only retained these until March 1946 when it disbanded at Koggala. Code was BN-

No 246 Sqn

No 246 Sqn formed at Bowmore on 1 September 1942, but disbanded on 30 April 1943. Codes were OY- and VU-

No 259 Sqn

No 259 Sqn began converting to the Sunderland on 9 March 1945, but disbanded on 30 April, passing its aircraft on to the South African Air Force's No 35 Sqn. No unit codes were used.

No 270 Sqn

No 270 Sqn at Apapa, Nigeria, converted to the Sunderland in December 1943, and disbanded there on 30 June 1945. No unit codes were used.

No 330 (Norwegian) Sqn

No 330 Sqn began trading its anachronistic Northrop N-3PB floatplanes (and a handful of Catalinas) for Sunderlands from 9 February 1943. The unit had left Iceland on 24 January 1943, arriving at Oban on 28 January. It moved to Sullom Voe on 12 July, where it remained until the end of the war, returning to Stavanger on 30 May 1945, and transferring to the Royal Norwegian Air Force on 21 November.

No 330's submarine claims included U-240, U-322 (shared) and U-387 (damaged). Submarine-killing aircraft used by No 330 were EJ155/O (U-387), JM667/V (U-240) and NJ188/G (U-322).

Code WH-

No 343 (French) Sqn

Following the Allied invasion of North Africa and the transfer of French forces to Allied control, 3E and 4E (*Flotille* 1) re-equipped with Sunderlands from July 1943, merging to form *Flotille* 7F in October 1943. No 343 Sqn formed from *Flotille* 7F on 29 November 1943. Moving between Dakar, Bathurst and Freetown, the unit transferred back to *Aéronavale* control on 27 November 1945 as *Flotille* 7FE. No unit codes were used.

No 422 Sqn RCAF

No 422 Sqn formed at Lough Erne on 2 April 1942 and received its first Sunderland that November, flying its first operational sortie with the aircraft on 1 March 1943. The unit moved to Bowmore on 8 May 1943 and to St Angelo on 3 November 1943, returning to what was by then Castle Archdale on 13 April 1944. It disbanded on 3 September 1945 at Bassingbourn, its personnel moving there from Pembroke Dock (to where the unit had moved on 4 November 1944).

No 422's submarine claims included U-470 and U-625. Submarine-killing aircraft used by No 422 were EK591/U (U-625) and JM712/S (U-470).

Codes were DG-, 2- and YI-

No 423 Sqn RCAF

No 423 Sqn was formed at Oban on 18 May 1942, receiving its first Sunderland in July and moving to Castle Archdale on 2 November 1942. The unit officially disbanded at Bassingbourn on 3 September 1945.

No 423's submarine claims included U-311, U-338 (damaged), U-456, U-484 (shared), U-489, U-610, U-672 (damaged) and U-921. Submarine-killing aircraft used by No 423 were W6006/3-G (U-456), W6008/H (U-338), DD859/G (U-489), DD862/A (U-311 and U-672), DD863/J (U-610), DW111/S (U-921) and ML825/D (U-484).

Code was AB-, briefly changing to 3-

No 461 Sqn RAAF

No 461 Sqn formed at Mount Batten on 25 April 1942, moving to Hamworthy Junction on 3 September and to Pembroke Dock on 20 April 1943. The unit disbanded on 20 June 1945, returning to Australia on 31 October 1945.

No 461's submarine claims included U-106, U-119 (shared damaged), U-270, U-332, U-385 (shared), U-415 (damaged), U-461 and U-571. Submarine-killing aircraft used by No 461 were W6077/U (U-461), DV698/M (U-106, U-332 and U-415), EK577/D (U-571), ML735/A (U-270), ML741/P (U-385) and P (U-119).

Codes were UT- and 2-

No 490 Sqn RNZAF

No 490 Sqn formed at Jui on 28 March 1943 and began re-equipping with Sunderlands in May 1944, using these until disbandment on 1 August 1945.

No 10 Sqn RAAF

No 10 Sqn RAAF received its first aircraft at Pembroke Dock on 11 September 1939. The unit moved to Mount Batten on 1 April 1940, then alternated between the two bases, spending May 1941-January 1942 at Pembroke Dock. The unit ceased operations on 1 June 1945 and disbanded on 26 October 1945.

The unit's submarine claims included U-26 (shared), U-71 (damaged), U-105 (damaged), U-119 (shared damaged), U-162 (damaged), U-243, U-426, U-454, U-465 (shared), U-563 (shared), *Argo*, *Reginaldo Guiliano* (damaged) and *Luigi Torello* (damaged). Submarine-killing aircraft used by No 10 (RAAF) were P9603/H (U-26), W3983/R (*Reginaldo Guiliano* and *Argo*), W3986/U (U-71, *Reginaldo Guiliano*), W3993/W (U-105, U-465), W3994/X (*Luigi Torello*), W4019/A (U-162), W4020/B (U-454), W4030/H (U-243), DV969/E (U-563), EK586/U (U-426) and F/ (U-119).

Codes were PB- and RB-

No 40 Sqn RAAF

Formed at Townsville on 31 March 1944, No 40 Sqn RAAF moved to Port Moresby on 30 April. No unit codes were used.

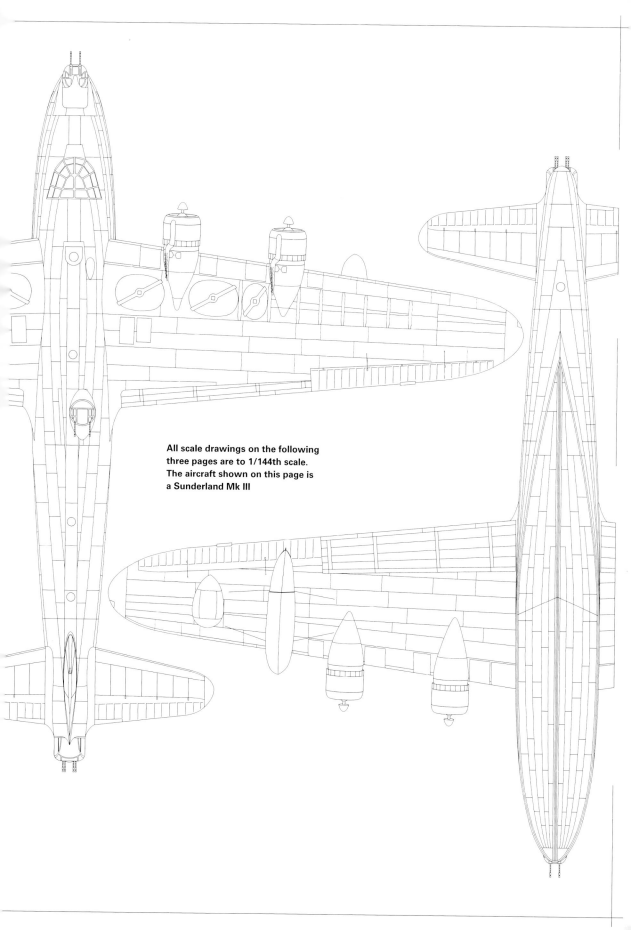

All scale drawings on the following
three pages are to 1/144th scale.
The aircraft shown on this page is
a Sunderland Mk III

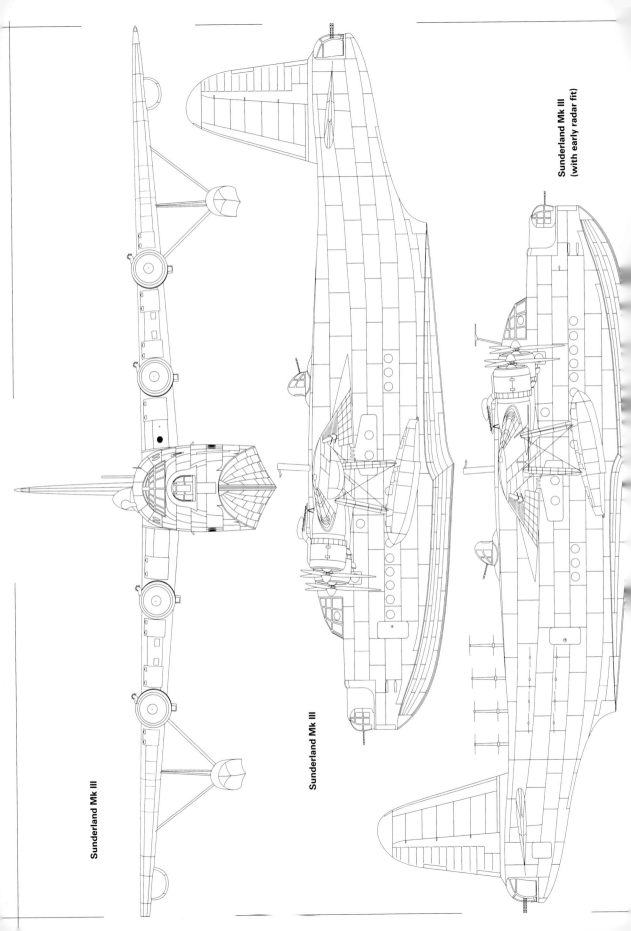

Sunderland Mk III

Sunderland Mk III

**Sunderland Mk III
(with early radar fit)**

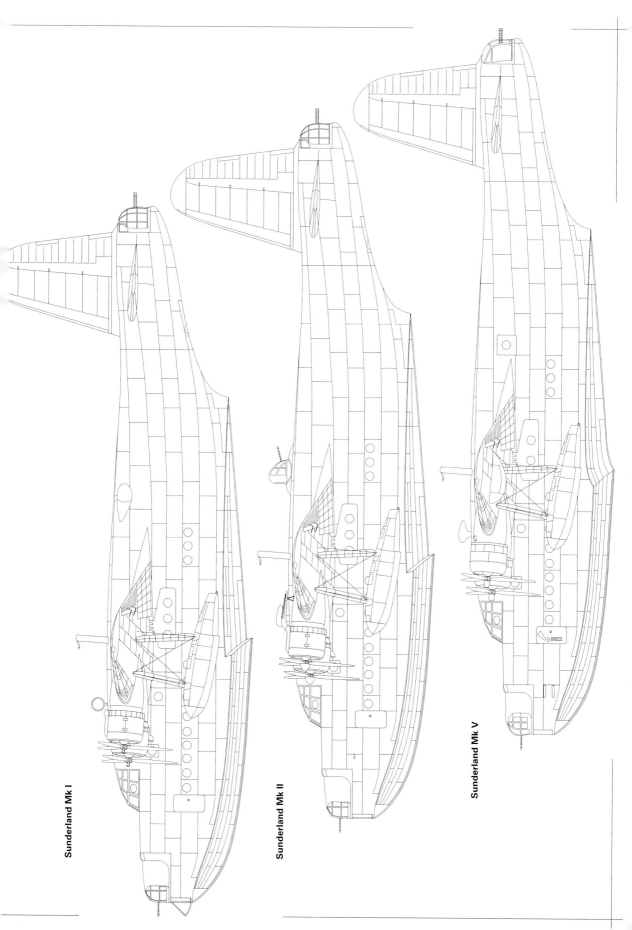

Sunderland Mk I

Sunderland Mk II

Sunderland Mk V

APPENDIX B

SUNDERLAND U-BOAT KILLS AND CLAIMS

U Boat	Type	Date	Sunderland	Result
U-26	IA	1/7/40	P9603/H, No 10 Sqn RAAF	Sunk, shared with RN ship
U-51	VIIB	16/8/40	P9624/H, No 210 Sqn	Damaged
U-55	VIIB	30/1/40	ML882/Y, No 228 Sqn	Sunk, shared with RN ships
U-71	VIIC	5/6/42	W3986/U, No 10 Sqn RAAF	Damaged, forced to RTB
U-105	IXB	11/6/42	W3993/W, No 10 Sqn RAAF	Damaged, forced into Spanish port
U-106	IXB	2/8/43	JM708/N, No 228 Sqn &	
			DV698/M, No 461 Sqn	Sunk
U-107	IXB	18/8/44	EJ150/W, No 201 Sqn	Sunk
U-119		29/4/43	P/No 461 & F/No 10 RAAF Sqns	Claimed damaged
U-162		11/7/42	W4019/A, No 10 Sqn RAAF	Damaged
U-240	VIIC	16/5/44	JM667/V, No 330 Sqn	Sunk, aircraft damaged, 2 crew dead
U-242		30/4/45	ML738/H, No 201 Sqn	Sunk, finished off by RN ships
U-243	VIIC	8/7/44	W4030/H, No 10 Sqn RAAF	Sunk
U-270	VIIC	12/8/44	ML735/A, No 461 Sqn	Sunk
U-297		6/12/44	N9025/Y, No 201 Sqn	Sunk, kill actually by RN ships
U-311		24/4/44	DD862/A, No 423 Sqn	Claimed sunk, actual victim U-672
U-322	VIIC	25/11/44	NJ188/G, No 330 Sqn	Called in RN ships to sink sub
U-332	VIIC	2/5/43	DV698/M, No 461 Sqn	Sunk
U-333	VIIC	11/6/44	ML880/U, No 228 Sqn	Damaged, Sunderland shot down
U-338		5/4/43	W6008/H, No 423 Sqn	Claimed sunk, actually damaged
U-383	VIIC	1/8/43	JM678/V, No 228 Sqn	Sunk
U-384		20/3/43	DD829/Z, No 202 Sqn	Sunk
U-385	VIIC	11/8/44	ML741/P, No 461 Sqn	Sunk, shared with RN ship
U-387	VIIC	19/7/44	EJ155/O, No 330 Sqn	Damaged
U-415	VIIC	1/5/43	DV698/M, No 461 Sqn	Damaged
U-426	VIIC	8/1/44	EK586/U, No 10 Sqn RAAF	Sunk
U-440	VIIC	31/5/43	DD835/R, No 201 Sqn	Sunk
U-441	VIIC	24/5/43	EJ139/L, No 228 Sqn	Damaged
U-454	VIIC	1/8/43	W4020/B, No 10 Sqn RAAF	Sunk, Sunderland shot down
U-456	VIIC	13/5/43	W6006/3-G, No 423 Sqn	Sunk
U-461	XIV	30/7/43	W6077/U, No 461 Sqn	Sunk
U-465	VIIC	7/5/43	W3993/W, No 10 Sqn RAAF	Sunk, shared with RN ship
U-470?		17/10/43	JM712/S, No 422 Sqn	Claimed damaged, Sunderland shot down
U-484	VIIC	11/9/44	ML825/D, No 423 Sqn	Claim shared with RCN ships
U-489	XIV	4/8/43	DD859/G, No 423 Sqn	Sunk, Sunderland shot down
U-518	IXC	27/6/43	W6005/P, No 201 Sqn	Damaged
U-527		20/3/43	DD829/Z, No 202 Sqn	Damaged
U-563	VIIC	31/5/43	DD838/X, No 228 Sqn &	
			DV969/E, No 10 Sqn RAAF	Sunk, shared with No 58 Sqn Halifax
U-564	VIIC	13/6/43	DV967/U, No 228 Sqn	Damaged, Sunderland shot down
U-564	VIIC	14/6/43	G/No 10 OTU	Sunk

U Boat	Type	Date	Sunderland	Result
U-571	VIIC	28/1/44	EK577/D, No 461 Sqn	Sunk
U-577	VIIC	9/1/42	W3987/X, No 230 Sqn	Sunk
U-607	VIIC	13/7/43	JM708/N, No 228 Sqn	Sunk
U-608		19/3/43	DD837/V, No 228 Sqn	Claimed damaged
U-610	VIIC	8/10/43	DD863/J, No 423 Sqn	Sunk
U-625	VIIC	10/3/44	EK591/U, No 422 Sqn	Sunk
U-631		20/3/43	W6051/T, No 201 Sqn	Actually U-384, as U-631 not sunk
U-672		24/4/44	DD862/A, No 423 Sqn	Severely damaged, claimed sunk
U-675	VIIC	24/5/44	ML736/R, No 4 OTU	Sunk
U-921	VIIC	24/5/44	DW111/S, No 423 Sqn	Several crew wounded, forced to RTB
U-955	VIIC	7/6/44	ML760/S, No 201 Sqn	Sunk
U-970	VIIC	7/6/44	ML877/R, No 228 Sqn	Sunk
U-995	VIIC	21/5/44	S/No 4 OTU (No 201 Sqn?)	Damaged, claimed sunk?
U-1222	IXC	11/7/44	ML881/P, No 201 Sqn	Sunk
Unidentified U-Boat		16/2/44	EK594/W, No 201 Sqn	Claimed damaged
Unidentified U-Boat		28/12/44	B/No 423 Sqn	Claimed damaged
Alabastro		14/9/42	W6002/R, No 202 Sqn	Sunk
Anfitrite		28/6/40	No 228 Sqn	Damaged
Argo		28/5/42	W3983/R, No 10 Sqn RAAF	Damaged, shared
Argonauta		28/6/40	L5804/S, No 230 Sqn	Sunk
Delfino		1/8/41	No 230 Sqn	Damaged, Sunderland shot down
Gondar		30/9/40	L2166, No 230 Sqn	Sunk, shared with RN ship
Reginaldo Guiliano		1/9/42	W3986/U & W3983/R, No 10 Sqn RAAF	Damaged, forced into Spanish port
Marcello		6/1/41	P9624/H, No 210 Sqn	Claimed sunk, actually lost in 2/41
Otaria		13/6/42	W4028/B, No 202 Sqn	Damaged
Rubino		29/6/40	L5804/S, No 230 Sqn	Sunk
Luigi Torello		7/6/42	W3994/X, No 10 Sqn RAAF	Damaged
Unidentified Italian		12/7/40	N9020, No 228 Sqn	Claimed sunk, no record of loss

Key

RN – Royal Navy
RCN – Royal Canadian Navy
RTB – Returned To Base

COLOUR PLATES

General Notes by the Artist

Early Sunderlands were painted an aluminium colour overall, although a small number of aircraft were also finished sky grey overall. In 1939 the Air Ministry stipulated that all flying boats should being painted in the Temperate sea scheme, which consisted of extra dark sea grey and dark slate grey, with aluminium or sky grey undersurfaces and medium sea grey squadron codes. This new scheme was first applied to Sunderlands in 1940, although some aircraft were also finished in dark green and medium sea grey. Reports also exist of a handful of aircraft camouflaged in dark green and dark earth during 1940-41, although hard photographic evidence to support this scheme has failed to come to light after much research for the profiles that appear in this book.

From mid-1940, the underside colour of the Sunderland changed from aluminium or sky grey to sky.

In July 1942 white was adopted as the underside colour for all RAF flying boats, this extending up the fuselage sides. Squadron codes also changed to slate grey at around this time.

In February 1943 the Temperate sea scheme for upper surfaces was replaced by extra dark sea grey. This colour faded very quickly, looking more like dark sea grey and, eventually, medium sea grey.

Australian-based Sunderlands were repainted foliage green overall, with bare metal planing surfaces below the chine. Finally, the RAAF's 'Empire' flying boats were almost certainly repainted with sky blue undersides and codes.

1
Sunderland GR 5 ML772/D of No 88 Sqn, Kai Tak, Hong Kong, 22 April 1949
No 88 Sqn was the only 'new' Sunderland unit formed after the end of the war, being created from No 1430 Flight at Kai Tak on 1 September 1946, and initially operating mainly in the transport role. The unit then assumed the General Reconnaissance mission and flew from Iwakuni for one year from June 1950, flying patrols along the Korean coastline during the Korean War. The unit was then used against Malayan terrorists during Operation *Firedog*, before disbanding on 1 October 1954 at Seletar, Singapore. On 21 April 1949 Flt Lt Ken Letford flew this aircraft (carrying doctors and medical supplies) to the frigate HMS *Amethyst* as it tried to run the Chinese blockade of the River Yangtse. Forced to abandon the attempt because when the vessel came under fire, the Sunderland returned that afternoon and dropped one RAF doctor before being forced to take off when it became the target of heavy machine gun fire. Another attempt to transfer a navy Chaplain

and replacement crew-members had to be abandoned the next day when the aircraft again drew heavy heavy fire as soon as it landed beside the frigate. Finally, on 23 April the Sunderland was forced to abort a reconnaissance flight after it was hit in a fuel tank, which was holed. Following repairs, the aircraft flew back to Kai Tak, having won its pilot a Bar to his DFC. ML772 remained with No 88 Sqn until the unit retired its Sunderlands in 1954. The flying boat was struck off charge on 30 June 1955.

2
Sunderland I L5802/SE-F of No 95 Sqn, Freetown, Sierra Leone, June 1941
Italy's entry into the war made the Mediterranean a more dangerous environment for merchant shipping, and increasing numbers of ships were sent in convoy around the Cape, with many convoys assembling at Freetown. Protection from U-Boats included No 95 Sqn, formed on 15 January 1941 from a detachment of three No 201 Sqn Sunderlands from Oban, which then built to squadron strength. The unit commenced operations on 24 March 1941, moving to Jui in April 1942 and to Bathurst in March 1943. The West African Sunderlands were modified with increased fuel tankage, but initially wore standard colours. 'SE-' and 'DQ-' code prefixes were used by No 95, which ceased flying on 25 May 1945, disbanding on 30 June. L5802 had served with Nos 210, 204 and 201 Sqns before joining No 95 Sqn, and went on to fly with No 461 Sqn and finally No 4 (Coastal) OTU. It was lost when it crashed at Alness whilst attempting a night landing on 16 January 1943.

3
Short S 23 C-Class AX659 of No 119 Sqn, Pembroke Dock, late June 1941
With its blunt, turretless nose, this C-Class 'Empire' flying boat never looked much like a Sunderland, although it was fully equipped with ASV radar, tail and mid-upper gun turrets and flew with Nos 119 and 201 Sqns. Formerly G-AETY with Imperial Airways, *Clio* was re-serialled as AX659 (sister-ship *Cordelia* becoming AX660) and remained in frontline service until it crashed on 22 August 1941. No 119 Sqn operated Sunderlands between September 1942 and April 1943 before disbanding at Pembroke Dock.

4
Short G-Class X8274 of No 119 Sqn, Pembroke Dock, May 1941
The G-Class flying boat was an enlarged derivative of the C-Class, with a Sunderland-type planing bottom. All three aircraft built (named *Golden Hind*, *Golden Fleece* and *Golden Horn*) were impressed into RAF service, serving with G Flight

(which became No 119 Sqn). Despite being allocated for VIP transport duties, this G-Class (formerly G-AFCJ *Golden Fleece* of Imperial Airways) was heavily armed, with an unusual unfaired tail turret and two tandem gun turrets on the spine. The tail turret was later more fully faired in, necessitating a reduction in rudder height. This aircraft was lost on 20 June 1941 when it ditched off Cape Finisterre and foundered.

5

Sunderland II W3981/ZM-W of No 201 Sqn, Castle Archdale, 28 October 1941

With its camouflaged upper surfaces and a very low demarcation between the topside colours and the undersides, W3981 was typical of early war Sunderlands. Although not fitted with a mid-upper gun turret, the aircraft had gun positions in hatches in the top of the fuselage, behind retractable fairings. The Mk II was also fitted with ASV antennas on the spine and sides of the rear fuselage, and below the outer wings. No 201 Sqn formed at Sullom Voe in June 1939, receiving its first Sunderlands on 13 April 1940. The unit moved to Invergordon on 4 June 1940, Lough Erne on 18 September and Castle Archdale on 9 October. W3981 survived both extensive frontline service (with Nos 201 and 240 Sqns) and a long spell in Training Command (with No 4 (Coastal) OTU), before being struck off charge on 1 July 1944.

6

Sunderland II W6055/ZM-R of No 201 Sqn, Castle Archdale, September 1942

Wearing the later Coastal Command colour scheme of white undersides and camouflaged top-sides, W6055 was fitted with a full suite of ASV radar antennas. It lacked a mid-upper gun turret, however, retaining the early faired gun positions. Captained by Flt Lt Doug Gall, W6055 was forced to beach at Benbecula on 27 September 1942. After eventual repair, the aircraft served with No 330 Sqn and survived the war, only to be scuttled in Loch Ryan on 11 December 1946. No 201 Sqn itself moved from Castle Archdale to Pembroke Dock, where it operated between March and November 1944, before returning to the former base. It moved back to Pembroke Dock on 3 August 1945, and remained here (apart from a brief stint at Calshot from April 1946 until January 1949) until the unit disbanded on 28 February 1957.

7

Sunderland GR V ML778/NS-Z of No 201 Sqn, Castle Archdale, 4 June 1945

No 201 Sqn's 'Z-Zebra' flew the last official convoy patrol of the war, on 3/4 June 1945, captained by Wg Cdr J Barrett of *Kensington Court* fame. ML778 had earlier flown with No 422 Sqn RCAF, in whose colours it is seen in profile No 28. It went on to fly with the *Aéronavale*. The RAF Museum's Sunderland is presently painted in the same codes, and ML824 is 'entitled' to wear these code letters as it had earlier served with No 201 Sqn as NS-Z – it was the unit's first GR V. The wartime 'NS-' code prefix was abandoned in April 1951.

8

Sunderland GR 5 VB889/NS-D of No 201 Sqn, Pembroke Dock (Operation *Plainfare*), 1948

VB889 was the last Sunderland serial allocated, this aircraft also being the last Blackburn-built Sunderland, leaving the company's Dumbarton factory in October 1945. The last Short-built aircraft was SZ599, which rolled off the Belfast line on 14 June 1946. VB889 participated in the Berlin Airlift, flying in and out of Lake Havel, wearing the individual code letter D with the unit's traditional 'NS-' code prefix. This aircraft carried the squadron's traditional badge above the cabin door. In 1953 VB889 was one of the three No 201 Sqn Sunderlands deployed to Britannia Lake to support the British North Greenland expedition. By then (August 1953) the aircraft carried the code prefix 'A' to the left of the roundel on each side. The alphabetical prefix was replaced by '201' before the Sunderland finally bowed out of service with this unit. VB889 later also served with No 88 Sqn and No 235 (Coastal) OCU, but was struck off charge on 8 August 1956 and sold for scrap on 20 September 1957.

9

Sunderland I N9046/KG-F of No 204 Sqn, Invergordon, 3 April 1940

On 3 April 1940, N9046 was probably the aircraft which earned the Sunderland its *'Fliegended Stachelschwein'* (flying porcupine) reputation, fighting off two, and then four and then another six Ju 88s which attempted to bomb a convoy it was escorting. Despite his aircraft having been badly damaged, with all tanks holed and several of the crew wounded, Flt Lt Frank Phillips nursed the aircraft home to a celebration – Cpl Lillie, in the tail turret, had shot down one of the Ju 88s and forced another to disengage, trailing thick smoke – this aircraft also failed to return to base. N9046 was eventually lost on 11 December 1940 when it caught fire at its moorings at Sullom Voe and burned out. No 204 Sqn had received its first Sunderland at Mount Batten on 8 June 1939 and flown its first operational sortie on 4 September. The unit moved to Sullom Voe (April 1940), Reykjavik (April 1941), Gibraltar (July 1941), Bathurst (August 1941) and Jui (January 1944), thereafter alternating between Jui and Bathurst until 30 June 1945, when it disbanded.

10

Sunderland GR 5 ML797/P of Nos 205/209 Sqns, Seletar, Singapore, 1959

Nos 205 and 209 Sqns were both long-serving Sunderland units in the Far East, equipping with the type during the war. Both continued to serve within the RAF postwar, and by late 1951 had been co-located at Seletar, Singapore. No 209 Sqn was disbanded into No 205 Sqn in January 1955, and for the rest of the Sunderland era, the remaining aircraft and aircrew were known as No 205/209 Sqn. DP198/W and ML797/P were the last aircraft on charge, DP198 flying the final 'op' on 14 May 1959, and ML797 leading a final formation flight the following day. ML797 (the RAF's last operational Sunderland) flew one last sortie on 20 May, and was then provisionally allocated for preservation. However, the lack of flying boat handling facilities between Singapore and the UK led to cancellation of these plans, and it was struck off charge on 30 June and sold for scrap locally.

11
Sunderland I L2163/DA-G of No 210 Sqn, Oban, 1940

No 210 Sqn was the RAF's first Sunderland unit (although not the first to receive a Sunderland), being issued with its first aircraft at Pembroke Dock on 3 July 1938. The unit moved to Tayport on 29 September and back to Pembroke Dock on 8 October, then to Invergordon on 23 October, where it remained until 13 July 1940, when a final move was made to Oban. The unit re-equipped with Catalinas in April 1941. Following service with No 210 Sqn, L2163 spent time with Nos 240 and 10 RAAF Sqn, before finally being written off on 15 January 1942 when driven ashore during a gale that struck its Stranraer base. The Sunderland was assigned to No 228 Sqn at the time.

12
Sunderland I N6135/TO-U of No 228 Sqn, Kalafrana, Malta, summer 1939

No 228 Sqn received its first Sunderland at Pembroke Dock in November 1938, and disbanded there on 4 June 1945. In the intervening period the unit had operaetd from Alexandria, Aboukir, Kalfrana, Aboukir again and Bathurst, before returning to Stranraer in October 1941. Thereafter, it flitted between Oban and Lough Erne, before settling back at Pembroke Dock in May 1943. Wearing the original Sunderland silver finish, N6135 carries no fin flash and has its serial number repeated on the rudder in peacetime style. The aircraft did have toned-down roundels on the fuselage, however, and 'TO-' codes, into which the fuselage serials 'fitted'. This aircraft's service with No 228 Sqn was briefly interrupted by a spell with No 210 Sqn in early 1939. It was written off in a landing accident at Pembroke Dock on 10 September 1939 at the end of a ferry flight from Malta.

13
Sunderland I N6138/TO-V of No 228 Sqn, Aboukir, July 1940

Even as late as mid-1940, some Sunderlands still wore their pre-war silver livery, like this aircraft of No 228 Sqn which was operating from Aboukir and Gibraltar, patrolling the North African coast to pinpoint the location of potentially hostile Vichy French naval units. Only the toned-down roundel and removal of the rudder serial mark this flying boat as being any different from pre-war Sunderlands. Initially operated by short-lived Sunderland operator No 202 Sqn between April and May 1939, this aircraft was transferred to No 228 Sqn. Surviving its frontline tour, N6138 was lost while in service with No 4 (Coastal) OTU when it sank after losing a float on landing at Alness on 17 July 1943.

14
Sunderland I N6135/BH-U of No 228 Sqn, Pembroke Dock, September 1939

This aircraft (also featured in profile No 12) still wears toned down roundels on its fuselage, red, white and blue roundels underwing and has no fin flash. However, the Sunderland has been painted sky grey overall, losing its squadron badge in the process. Strangely, the prewar practice of repeating the aircraft's serial on the rudder has been observed following its repainting. Note too that the squadron's code letters have changed from 'TO-' to 'BH-', although the former combination reappeared in 1940 – see profile 13.

15
Sunderland II W3989/DQ-L of No 228 Sqn, Lough Erne, December 1942

This late Sunderland II featured ASV radar, which was fitted in conjunction with the faired gun positions in the upper fuselage. No 228 Sqn moved from Oban to Lough Erne on 11 December 1942, taking this aircraft with it. It wears standard camouflage for the period, but with a long curving demarcation line between the upper surface colours and the undersides on the rear fuselage. W3989 shuttled back and forth between Nos 202 and 228 Sqns, then flew with No 4 (Coastal) OTU and No 302 FTU. It was struck off charge on 23 February 1945.

16
Sunderland III ML770/1-P of No 228 Sqn, Pembroke Dock, 1944

No 228 Sqn disbanded as a Sunderland unit on 4 June 1945, subsequently re-equipping with Liberators in the transport role. Unusually, this Sunderland carried nose-art (in the form of a cartoon of 'P/O Prune') above the door, although this was later removed on the orders of the unit's then CO, Wg Cdr Lombard. Another No 228 Sqn aircraft with nose-art was W4026 1-M, which carried a boxing kangaroo motif. This latter aircraft, captained by Flt Lt Frank Goyen, was the one in which the Duke of Kent was killed on 25 August 1942, en route from Invergordon to Iceland. ML770 (which served exclusively with No 228 Sqn) was also lost in service, hitting a rock while taxying after landing off the Scilly Isles on 21 February 1945.

17
Sunderland I L2160 *Selangor* of No 230 Sqn, Seletar, Singapore, October 1938

This aircraft (the third production Sunderland) was the second Short flying boat issued to No 230 Sqn, being flown out to Seletar by Sqn Ldr Watts-Read and the unit's CO, Wg Cdr G M Bryer OBE, AFC. Born in 1897, Bryer had met Cody and Bleriot as a 15-year-old boy, and subsequently joined the Royal Naval Air Service, with whom he pioneered deck landings in Sopwith Pups. This aircraft was named *Selangor* at Port Swettenham by the State of Selangor's Sultan in October 1938, and a further three squadron Sunderlands were christened *Pahang*, *Perak* and *Negri Sembilan* after neighbouring Federated Malay States at much the same time. This acknowledged the £2.5 m fund provided by the Sultans of those states to the Imperial Government to cover the cost of two squadrons of aircraft for the defence of Malaya. This substantial amount naturally more than covered the cost of the Sunderlands. The name *Selangor* was placed on the nose in Malay script, while the unit's Tiger and Palm Tree badge was carried in a star-shaped frame on the nose. The aircraft was finished in high-speed silver, with red white and blue roundels, no fin flash and the serial repeated on the rudder.

18
Sunderland I N9029/NM-V of the No 230 Sqn Detachment at Scaramanga, 1941

On 27 March 1941, N9029, captained by Flt Lt Alan Lywood, shadowed the Italian Fleet prior to the Battle of Cape Matapan in which HMS *Formidable*, HMS *Warspite* and other British ships (and *Formidable*'s aircraft) sank three Italian cruisers and damaged the battleship *Vittorio Veneto*. During April 1941, the Sunderlands of Nos 228 and 230 Sqns at Alexandria had been heavily engaged in evacuating forces from Yugoslavia to Greece in the face of the German onslaught. Following the collapse of Yugoslavia it became clear that Greece itself could not hold out, and the aircraft were then committed to evacuating troops from mainland and island Greece to Crete, and then from Crete to North Africa. The Sunderlands were augmented by BOAC's C-Class boats *Cambria* (G-ADUV) and *Coorong* (G-AEVI). During the brief campaign, the Sunderlands evacuated some 1096 men, and transported tons of valuable supplies. This aircraft was unusual in having camouflage that wrapped around the rear fuselage. The Sunderland wore a huge rectangular red white and blue fin flash, with each stripe being of equal proportions. N9029 was lost on an anti-submarine patrol some 100 miles north of the Egyptian port of Damietta on New Year's Day 1943, still coded NM-V.

19
Sunderland III (serial unknown)/R of No 230 Sqn, Koggala, Ceylon, 1944

This No 230 Sqn Sunderland wore standard SEAC roundel, and fin flashes, but its colour scheme had faded badly by the time it was seen in the co-located Maintenance Unit (MU) at Koggala. Indeed, it was so weathered that its serial was almost illegible. It is impossible to say with any confidence whether the aircraft had a single topside colour, or if two colours had become indistinguishable. The Sunderland had no mid upper turret, but was fitted with ASV spines.

20
Sunderland III JM711/M of No 230 Sqn, Koggala, Ceylon, 1944

JM711 was in the Koggala MU at the same time as the aircraft featured in the previous profile, and wore a colour scheme with a similar demarcation line, although this had not faded. Most of the unit's aircraft at that time wore the normal Coastal Command grey topped with white colour scheme, thus leaving JM711 and the unidentified Mk III very much in the minority. This aircraft was struck off charge in August 1946 following a spell with the Iraq Communications Flight.

21
Sunderland III JM659/Q of No 230 Sqn, operating behind enemy lines in Burma, June 1944

In June 1944, two No 230 Sqn Sunderlands (coded 'O' and 'Q') participated in a historic large scale evacuation of wounded Chindits after a major offensive. The aircraft flew to and from Indawagyi Lake for 32 days, lifting a total of 537 men, many of whom would otherwise have died. Indawagyi Lake was, like the Chindits HQ at Mokso, miles behind enemy lines, but the Sunderland operation was conducted without being discovered by the Japanese, until on the last day an enemy fighter made an unsuccessful strafing attack on 'O' as it sat on the Lake. 'Q' had by then been written off at her moorings at Dibrugarh, on the Brahmaputra River, on 4 July during a hurricane that swept through the region. The Chindit troops christened the two Sunderlands (captained by Flt Lts Garside and Rand) 'Gert' and 'Daisy' after a pair of famous music hall characters.

22
Sunderland III ML868/H of No 230 Sqn, Koggala, Ceylon, October 1944

Like most of No 230 Sqn's Sunderlands, ML868 wears standard Coastal Command colours, although the unit did have a significant minority of aircraft with decidedly 'non-standard' schemes. This aircraft was typical in being fitted with the 'Stickleback' type ASV antenna array, but was less typical within No 230 Sqn in retaining a mid upper turret. By this stage of the war, enemy air opposition was rare in the Indian Ocean, and the mid-upper turret was regarded as an unwelcome source of unnecessary weight, drag and complexity. Plans to simply replace them with a fixed timber fairing were looked upon askance by some engineers within No 230 Sqn, who devised a jettisonable perspex escape hatch which they manufactured and cleared, and which eventually formed the basis of a fleet-wide modification. Built by Blackburn Aircraft at the company's Dumbarton factory in early 1944, this particular aircraft served throughout its frontline career with No 230 Sqn. It was struck off charge on 31 January 1946.

23

Sunderland III JM673/P 'Black Peter' of No 230 Sqn, Koggala, Ceylon, October 1944

Coded 'P-for-Peter', JM673 was painted in a non-standard black colour scheme for use in dawn and dusk attacks on enemy shipping in the Bay of Bengal, but retained standard blue/off-white SEAC national insignia. Equipped with ASV radar, JM673 lacked a mid-upper gun turret, the latter having been deleted to save weight and reduce drag. The aircraft became the personal mount of squadron OC, Wg Cdr Dundas K Bednall, but was lost while being flown by Sqn Ldr K V Ingham RAAF after Bednall had been posted away. JM673 failed to return after a weather-recall was issued on 28 November 1944, squadron personnel watching its 'radar blip' heading directly towards that of a massive cyclone off the Ceylonese coast.

24

Sunderland III ML867/N of No 270 Sqn, Apapa, Nigeria, 1944

Nigeria-based No 270 Sqn replaced its Catalinas with Sunderland IIIs from 5 December 1943, and used them for patrols off West Africa until 30 June 1945, when the unit disbanded. This aircraft (in common with some others on the squadron) wore an oversized code letter, and was struck off charge on 21 June 1945.

25

Sunderland III ML814/WH-A of No 330 (Norwegian) Sqn, Sullom Voe, April 1945

The Norwegian flag over the cabin door identifies this Sunderland III as an aircraft of No 330 Sqn, which it joined in April 1945 after service with Nos 201 and 422 Sqns. No 330 Sqn re-equipped with Sunderlands in February 1943, and operated these from Oban and Sullom Voe until May 1945, when it transferred to Stavanger – it passed back to Royal Norwegian Air Force control that November. ML814 subsequently returned to the UK and was eventually sold to the RNZAF. After service in New Zealand as NZ4109, it was crudely civilianised in Australia and flown by Ansett as VH-BRF from 1963, and then Antilles Air Boats as N158J. It was finally returned to Britain in March 1981, flying briefly as G-BJHS. The aircraft was subsequently damaged in the hurricane that struck southern England in October 1987, and after restoration to flying condition, was flown across the Atlantic to join the collection of Kermit Weeks in Florida, where it remains to this day.

26

Sunderland GR V ML824/WH-T of No 330 (Norwegian) Sqn, Sullom Voe, 1944

Like ML814, this surviving Sunderland eventually found a berth with the Norwegian-manned No 330 Sqn, again after serving with No 201 Sqn (as NS-Z – the markings it now wears in the Battle of Britain wing at RAF Hendon Museum). After withdrawal from service, the aircraft was sold to France, and served with the *Aéronavale* until 1960. After the failure of the RAF to fly a Seletar-based Sunderland back to the UK for preservation, it was left to the French to display their customary flair and creativity, and they did so in spades. ML824 was given free to the British Government for presentation to the Sunderland Trust, and was flown back from Dakar, West Africa to Brest, and then onwards to Pembroke Dock. It arrived here on 24 March 1961, and was 'preserved' in this location, deteriorating badly, for the next ten years. ML824 was finally transferred to the new RAF Museum at Hendon in 1971.

27

Sunderland III ML884/DG-Z of No 422 Sqn RCAF, Pembroke Dock, 8 December 1944

No 422 Sqn (known as the 'Flying Yachtsmen') formed at Lough Erne on 2 April 1942, and received its first Sunderland on 1 November 1942. The unit moved to Oban (November 1942), Bowmore (May 1943), St Angelo (November 1943) and Castle Archdale (April 1944), before settling at Pembroke Dock on 4 November 1944. Newly-painted rectangles behind the G and Z of ML884's codes indicate a recent re-coding, with retention of the initial D perhaps indicating a transfer from co-located No 228 Sqn, although ML884's individual record card gives no hint of this. Used exclusively by No 422 Sqn, the aircraft was struck off charge on 26 March 1947.

28

Sunderland III ML778/2-S of No 422 Sqn RCAF, Pembroke Dock, 8 December 1944

Illustrated as it appeared on the same day as ML884, ML778 wears the later '2-' code prefix used by both Nos 422 and 461 Sqns at Pembroke Dock in late 1944 and early 1945. After service with No 422 'Flying Yachtsmen' Sqn, ML778 eventually reached No 201 Sqn, with whom it flew the last convoy patrol of the war, and in whose markings it is illustrated in profile 7. No 422 Sqn finished the war having flown 1116 operational sorties, for the loss of nine aircraft and 42 aircrew killed.

29

Sunderland III DV960/2-H of No 461 Sqn, Mount Batten, 26 July 1942

Australian-manned No 461 Sqn formed in April 1942 from a nucleus provided by No 10 Sqn RAAF, the new unit flying its first 'op' on 1 July 1942. Salt spray and weather could wreak havoc on an aircraft's carefully applied paint, and this No 461 Sqn Sunderland III already looks well overdue for a return visit to the paint shop. DV960 was duly passed on to No 131 (Coastal) OTU and was struck off charge on 31 May 1945.

30

Sunderland GR V RN282/UT-N of No 461 Sqn, Pembroke Dock, 1945

After being based at Hamworthy junction between September 1942 and April 1943, No 461 Sqn moved to Pembroke Dock, where it saw out the rest of the war. The unit officially disbanded on 20 June 1945 and returned to Australia in October. The war cost No 461 Sqn the lives of 86 aircrew killed in action and 14 aircraft. This Sunderland was unusual in having its white undersides extending to cover the wing and tailplane leading edges and the whole of the engine cowlings – a colour scheme which only became common postwar. RN282 was finally struck off charge on 13 May 1958, having flown with Nos 10 RAAF, 201, 88, 209 and 205 Sqns during a frontline career that had lasted 13 years.

31
Sunderland GR 5 NJ205/TA-F of No 235 (Coastal) OCU, Calshot, 1948

Used briefly as a Sunderland aircrew trainer, the still very new NJ205 later became Solent 3 G-AKNS *City of Liverpool* with BOAC. Prior to its civilianisation, the aircraft had participated in Operation *Plainfare* (the Berlin Airlift) with other No 235 (Coastal) OCU flying boats. G-AKNS was finally scrapped at Hamworthy in 1954.

32
Sunderland III 'Hythe Class' G-AGHW *Hamilton*, BOAC, Hythe, Southampton, 1943

Wartime attrition of the Short C- and G-Class flying boats led to the transfer of some 26 Sunderlands to BOAC, with relatively minor modifications to fit them for the transport role. The transferred aircraft were hastily camouflaged in grey and green, with black serials thinly outlined in silver underlined with a red, white and blue stripe, and with a silver-edged 'Speedbird' on the nose. Sunderland ML725 was transferred to BOAC to become G-AGHW *Hamilton* on 27 August 1943, and finally crashed whilst still in BOAC service in November 1947. Some of the transferred Sunderland IIIs became 'Hythes' (with a less austere interior) after the war, and other Sunderlands were returned to Shorts to be rebuilt as Sandringhams. The later aircraft featured a re-shaped nose and tail fairing and a luxurious interior, which included a cocktail lounge, ladies powder room, linen room and dining saloon, and with provision for eight bunks. The Sandringham 2 had Pratt & Whitney Twin Wasp engines, while the Seaford-based Solent was similarly powered, but offered higher take off weights and more spacious accommodation.

33
Seaford NJ201/OZZA, BOAC

The Hercules-engined Seaford was designed for service in the Pacific, but performance was disappointing, and with the end of the war production was cut back to only eight aircraft. After trials with No 201 Sqn, most were converted to Solent configuration for service with BOAC. This Seaford wears standard RAF Coastal Command grey and white maritime camouflage, but with a dark blue 'Speedbird' on the nose and the Transport Command code OZZA in black on the rear fuselage. Most Seafords were

subsequently stripped of paint and ASV equipment and fitted with Sandringham-style nose and tail fairings, thereby becoming Solents with BOAC. NJ201 was temporarily registered as G-AGWU and loaned to BOAC for evaluation in December 1945. It was eventually fully converted to Solent 2 configuration as G-ANAJ *City of Funchal*, serving with Aquila Airways until wrecked in a gale on 26 September 1956.

34
Sunderland I P9605/RB-K of No 10 Sqn RAAF, Pembroke Dock, 1941

No 10 Sqn was formed at Point Cook on 1 July 1939, and a detachment from the unit was attached to No 210 Sqn at Pembroke Dock in August 1939, with seven pilots going to Calshot for type conversion. This was to allow No 10 Sqn's crews to familiarise themselves with the newly-purchased Sunderlands, which were then to be flown south to Australia. The unit's intended base was Rathmines, on Lake McQuarrie, in New South Wales. However, when war broke out, it was decided that No 10 Sqn would remain in the UK and carry on the fight from there. The unit received its first Sunderland on 11 September 1939, and was declared operational on 1 February 1940. Following extensive service with No 10 Sqn RAAF, P9605 moved to No 4 (Coastal) OTU, with whom it was damaged on 20 October 1943 and subsequently broken up for spares.

35
Sunderland III W3999/RB-Y of No 10 Sqn RAAF, Mount Batten, early 1942

W3999 was the first production Sunderland III, and made it maiden flight on 15 December 1941. The aircraft served in this 'Stickleback' configuration with these markings while operated by No 10 Sqn RAAF, and during trials at the MAEE at Helensburgh. It was shot down by an Arado Ar 196 on 21 June 1942 over the Bay of Biscay. No 10 Sqn RAAF (with its off-shoot, No 461) participated in the sinking of 12 U-Boats, and drove forward many Sunderland modifications and improvements, not the least of which was the re-engining of the Mk III, which directly resulted in production of the definitive wartime Sunderland, the Mk V.

36
Sunderland III W4004/Z of No 10 Sqn RAAF, Mount Batten, 17 May 1943

This very heavily weathered Sunderland III was lost, along with captain Flt Lt K McKenzie and his crew, on 17 May 1943. The demarcation line between the upper surface disruptive camouflage and the white undersides was in the early, lower position, and the white paint in particular was extremely badly weathered and worn. No 10 Sqn RAAF fought on until 7 May 1945 (its last wartime op), and ceased operations on 1 June, finally disbanding on 26 October 1945. During the war it had flown 3239 sorties and suffered no fewer than 151 fatalities.

37
S 33 C-Class A18-14/DQ-B of No 41 (Sea Transport) Sqn RAAF, Townsville, Queensland, early 1943

The Short S 30 had introduced Bristol Perseus engines, which developed less power than the Pegasus, but which were fitted in narrower, lower drag nacelles, giving a slight edge in performance. They were also cleared for higher All Up Weights (46,000-lb for take off and 53,000 lb after inflight refuelling), and were equipped with air-to-air refuelling gear. The last two 'Empires' built reverted to the Pegasus, and were cleared only to the original 40,500-lb All Up Weight, and were known as S 33s. BOAC's G-AFPZ *Clifton* was one of the latter, the aircraft being depicted here after it had joined No 41 (Sea Transport) Sqn – whose codes it wears – from No 33 Sqn. Although originally operated with standard RAF roundels and fin flash (see profile 39), the S 33 gained RAAF dull blue and white roundels and fin flash with its new unit, and its undersides were repainted in sky blue. Unusually, roundels were not applied under the wings, and nor were serial numbers. Defences were limited to two gun positions in the roof-mounted escape hatches. The last of five 'Empire' boats acquired by the RAAF (on 9 March 1942), this aircraft was passed on to QANTAS on 15 June 1943.

38
Sunderland III A26-6 of No 40 Sqn RAAF, Townsville, Queensland, Summer 1944

During the prewar expansion of the RAAF, plans were made for the establishment of two flying boat units (Nos 10 and 11 Sqns) equipped initially with nine Sunderlands, allocated serials A18-1 to A18-9. These aircraft were diverted to meet RAF orders, while No 10 Sqn (having moved to Britain for Sunderland conversion) ended up staying in the UK to fight in the European theatre of operations. Despite the particular unsuitability of the Sunderland for tropical operations, a number were used by units based in Australia itself, and six were eventually delivered (as A26-1 to A26-6)

for use by No 40 Sqn from June 1944. Although fitted with ASV, the Australian-based Sunderlands operated mainly as transports, until they ceased flying in March 1946 after completing 1613 sorties, totalling 7097 flying hours. This particular aircraft was written off after colliding with a dolphin in Townsville's harbour entrance in November 1944. The remaining five flying boats survived the rigours of wartime life, and were eventually sold to Trans Ocean Airways in 1947.

39
S 33 C-Class A18-14 of No 33 Sqn RAAF, Townsville, Queensland, Summer 1942

Also illustrated in profile 37, A18-14 is depicted here during the brief time it spent with No 33 Sqn, prior to being passed on to No 41 Sqn. It wears extra dark sea grey and dark slate grey disruptive camouflage on its top surfaces, standard RAF-type roundels but no squadron codes.

40
Sunderland III NZ4101 *TAINUI* of the Flying Boat Transport Flight, RNZAF, March 1945

Crews who had flown Sunderlands with No 490 Sqn ferried four Sunderland IIIs to New Zealand in late 1944. These subsequently formed the Sunderland Flying Boat Section, and were operated mainly in the freight role. The unit (soon redesignated as the Flying Boat Transport Flight) undertook scheduled services to Espiritu Santo, Fiji and Sydney. In November 1945 it was redesignated once again, becoming the Sunderland Flying Boat Transport Squadron. By March 1945 NZ4101's paintwork was looking shabby and well-worn, and the RAF-type C roundels were flanked by blue-edged white bars – note also the name *TAINUI* applied above the cabin door. Soon after the war, the Sunderlands were stripped to bare metal finish and fitted with de Havilland fully-feathering propellers. They were sold off to civil operators in 1947, and had been scrapped by the time the RNZAF took delivery of its 16 re-conditioned MR 5s from June 1953.

SELECTED BIBLIOGRAPHY

Ashworth, Chris, *RAF Coastal Command 1936-1969*. PSL, 1992
Banks, Arthur, *Wings of the Dawning*. Images Publishing, 1996
Barnes, C H, *Shorts Aircraft since 1900*. Putnam, 1967
Bowyer, Chaz, *The Sunderland at War*. Ian Allan, 1976
Bowyer, Chaz, *The Short Sunderland*. Aston, 1989
Bowyer, Chaz, *Coastal Command at War*. Ian Allan, 1979
Bowyer, Michael J F, *RAF Camouflage of World War Two*. PSL 1975
Hendrie, Andrew, *Short Sunderland in World War II*. Airlife, 1994
Evans, John, *The Sunderland Flying Boat Queen*. Paterchurch, 1995
Franks, Norman, *Conflict over the Bay*. Grub St, 1999
Franks, Norman and Zimmerman, Eric, *U-Boat versus Aircraft*. Grub St, 1998)
Norris, Geoffrey, *The Short Sunderland*. Profile Publications, 1967
Norris, Geoffrey, *The Short Empire Boats*. Profile Publications, 1966
Rance, Adrian B, *Seaplanes and Flying Boats of the Solent*. Southampton University, 1981